CERAMICS
FOR GARDENS
& LANDSCAPES

KARIN HESSENBERG

First published in Great Britain 2000
by A & C Black (Publishers) Limited,
35 Bedford Row, London WC1R 4JH

ISBN 0 7136 4704 3

Copyright © 2000 Karin Hessenberg

Published simultaneously in the USA by Krause Publications, Iola, Wis.

ISBN 0-87341-578-7

Designed by Sharyn Troughton
Cover design by Dorothy Moir

Illustrations:
Front cover: (clockwise from top left): Green birdbath by Karin Hessenberg;
Planter by Andrea Wulff (detail); Terracotta flowerpots by John Huggins;
Fish by Kate Malone (detail)
Title page: Tall pots by Monica Young exhibited at Hannah Peschar
Sculpture Garden. *Photo: Hannah Peschar*

Printed and bound in Singapore by Tien Wah Press Limited.

CONTENTS

ACKNOWLEDGEMENTS

I would like to thank all the potters and artists who have contributed to this book and without whom it would not have been possible.

I would also like to thank my photographers, and the staff at the British Museum, City of Stoke-on-Trent Museum, at Royal Doulton, the Crafts Council and other crafts organisations, gallery directors and magazine editors who have provided me with pictures and invaluable help with my research.

Finally, I would like to thank my husband for his help with the book in many ways, in particular reading the text and for his patience while I wrote it.

The following photographs were taken by the author: pp. 8 top left; 12; 24; 29; 58 top right; group on top left; 60; 87 bottom; 118; 123; 124; 125.

PREFACE

When I set out to write this book, it was because I thought that the open air environment was one which had been overlooked by ceramics practitioners, critics and galleries. I found that many artists and potters were making a great variety of work for gardens and landscapes, but were under-represented in galleries, perhaps because of the large size of the work. However, this cannot be the reason for the dearth of critical comment, and I hope that this book will show that there are many artists producing interesting work for the open air. In the Appendix I have listed some exhibition venues and I recommend that critics visit them more frequently than they do at present.

When displaying ceramic objects in the open, many factors have to be taken into consideration, including weather resistance, safety, durability and coping with heavy weights. These factors are discussed in 'Practical Considerations', at the back of the book. Any working practices which particular makers have devised, whether it is a specially adapted kiln or their own invented tools, are described in the section covering that potter's techniques. Processes which are commonly used by makers are described in 'Practical Considerations' and illustrated with notes and examples from individual makers.

I have deliberately not described techniques such as coiling or throwing as these have been extensively covered in other books. However, where such a technique has been modified to make large objects, it has been described and I have included a considerable amount of detail on throwing very large pots.

While this book is about present day potters and artists, I have included some history of the development of gardens, particularly in Britain. This is because the fortunes of pots and garden ornaments have been closely linked with the development and fashion of gardens. The current wave of interest in gardening has provided great scope for makers of ceramics, whether it is for thrown pots in a traditional mode or for abstract sculpture. I hope that this book goes a little way towards showing the many ways in which ceramics can relate to plants, gardens and landscapes.

ABOVE: Ancient Egyptian garden with pond shown in a wall painting fragment from the tomb of Nebamun.
Photo: Courtesy of The British Museum.

BELOW: Assyrian stone relief panel showing Ashurbanipal and his queen banqueting in a garden.
Photo: Courtesy of The British Museum.

INTRODUCTION

Early Beginnings

Pottery has been associated with gardens from the earliest times and while the popularity of ornaments has waxed or waned with changing garden fashions, the functional plant pot has endured. Archaeological evidence shows that the ancient Egyptians cultivated gardens. They grew plants in brick containers and pots which they filled with fertile mud from the banks of the River Nile to protect the roots from drying out in the sandy desert soil. Tomb paintings depict formal gardens with ponds and ornamental trees, and the Pharoah Rameses III (1200 BC) is known to have grown trees and shrubs in decorated earthenware containers. Potted plants were usually arranged in straight lines or placed on corners to emphasize the symmetry of the garden.

Like the Egyptians, the Assyrians of Mesopotamia (825–600BC) lived in an arid region, where they depended on the waters of the Tigris and Euphrates rivers. They too prized gardens with water, trees and scented flowers. The Hanging Gardens of Babylon built by Nebuchadnezzar were constructed on a stone-vaulted base in a series of terraces which were irrigated by a hydraulic system. Such gardens were designed for pleasure, as shown in the carving of Ashurbanipal and his Queen being entertained by musicians in a garden.

The Assyrians had close links with the Persians who laid out formal gardens based on the idea of the four elements – earth, air, fire and water. The Persian gardens were symmetrical and pots were important accessories standing at the intersection of paths or on the edge of a canal or rectangular pond. The pots were simple and undecorated and the Persians used them in large quantities to mass together flowers chosen for their scent. Persian gardens have not only provided the basis of garden design throughout the Islamic world – as seen in the Mughal gardens of India or the Moorish gardens of Spain – but they have also indirectly influenced the design of Western gardens.

Greek travelers brought back descriptions of fabulous gardens in Persia, Assyria and Egypt. When Lysander, an envoy from Greece, went to the court of Cyrus of Persia (559–529BC), he was amazed that Cyrus had laid out his own garden, since the Greeks regarded martial arts rather than gardening as suitable pursuits for men. In Persia, gardening was considered a noble activity and it was an essential part of the education of kings as it was thought to develop wisdom.

The Greeks were rather slow to develop ornamental gardens, although Athens had shady groves of trees under which philosophers held discussions, and there were gardens associated with gymnasia and temples. Excavations of ancient Greek houses show that most domestic gardens were in fact courtyards where plants were grown in pots.

The Mediterranean garden style, with classical statues, topiary and colonnades, was really

Pots of flowers massed together in an Islamic garden at the Alhambra, Granada, Spain.
Photo: Robin Parrish.

founded by the Romans who had a great variety of gardens in which they cultivated fruit trees and herbs. Domestic gardens were usually planted in courtyards to provide food for the household, but with the increasing wealth of the Roman Empire the aristocracy built themselves fine villas with ornamental gardens, which often featured formal ponds and colonnades. The geometric style echoed the symmetry of Persian gardens. The Romans grew many kinds of plants in pots, including orange and lemon trees.

There were flowers in Roman gardens, but much of the color was provided by mosaics, painted statuary and colored marble. The painted walls of villas at Pompeii provide some of the best surviving records of Roman gardens.

Roman mosaic from Halikarnassus showing an acanthus plant growing in a *krater* pot.
Photo: Courtesy of The British Museum.

8

View of the colonnade of the Canopus at Hadrian's Villa in Tivoli, Italy.

Gardens in Europe and Britain 1500–1850

Gardens declined in Europe after the collapse of the Roman Empire but Roman garden designs were revived in the villa gardens of Italy in the 15th century. In this period there was a renaissance of terracotta production in Italy and all kinds of decorated pots, ornaments, mythical beasts and grotesque heads were made for these gardens.

Classical Roman style garden in the Alcazaba in Seville, Spain.
Photo: Robin Parrish.

Medieval Britain was relatively isolated from Europe and British gardens had a different style. Pottery had both a functional and an ornamental role in these gardens. Pots of scented plants such as lilies, pinks, or juniper would be placed in arbors or on grassy seats where people could sit next to them.

Many European elements of garden design came to Britain later, largely as a result of the invention of the printing press, and by the 16th century a range of pattern and design books for garden ornaments had been published. The large ornamental pots popular in the 17th century originated in Holland, although many were copied from Italian designs. English potters in turn copied these Italian style vases and urns and tried to establish their own market.

The English climate necessitated frostproof wares and this led to the invention of ceramic materials like Coade stone which was very durable and proved particularly suitable for making sculptures (see Chapter 9).

The Italianate garden went out of fashion in England in the 18th century under the influence of the garden designer Capability Brown and his concept of the natural landscape garden. Statues and ornamental pots were swept away and plant pots survived only as utilitarian items for germinating and propagating plants. However, the expansion of the British Empire and travel to distant parts of the world ensured the survival of

Italianate fountain in Regent's Park, London.
Photo: Robin Parrish.

At Versailles, France, palm trees are grown in tubs so that they can be taken indoors in the winter.
Photo: Robin Parrish.

large plant pots because collectors brought back specimens of plants previously unknown in Europe. Newly wealthy people who had made their money overseas built heated greenhouses to grow tropical fruit such as pineapples. Orangeries became popular and had their heyday in the 18th and 19th centuries. Citrus trees, which were grown in large pots, could be moved outside in the summer and taken back into the orangery for the winter. All of these changes in style took place in the large gardens and estates of wealthy merchants and the aristocracy.

The development of British garden styles from 1850 to the present

The domestic garden as we know it today is a 19th century development. With industrialization and the rise of the middle class came the rapid expansion of cities with suburban houses and town gardens. At the same time, new inventions changed the shape of gardens. The ability to manufacture plate glass, combined with the abolition of a tax on glass, resulted in a proliferation of conservatories and greenhouses. The lawnmower was being mass-produced by the 1850s and the lawn took on a central position in gardens. The introduction of rubber hoses and a piped water supply took the

A suburban garden of the 1920s with flower borders and sundial.
Photo: E. J. Hessenberg.

labor out of watering the garden. This resulted in the decline of stone and lead water tanks from which watering cans were once filled.

Mass production in the 19th century meant that a huge range of decorative items for middle-class gardens could be obtained at relatively modest prices. The Victorians copied many kinds of classical containers and ornaments such as statues, seats, tiles, fountains and bed edgings and manufactured them in cast iron, lead, stone or terracotta. Pottery manufacturers such as

Minton & Co. in Staffordshire and Doulton of Lambeth produced decorative terracotta garden ornaments such as elaborate vases, planters on pedestals, large colorful conservatory center-pieces in imitation majolica glaze and a variety of glazed fountains. Ceramic fountains are featured in Chapter 6 and garden furniture and tiles in Chapters 7 and 8 respectively.

Sundials, birdbaths (see Chapter 5) and statues were especially fashionable ornaments in Victorian gardens, although the statues were relatively small compared with those that formerly graced the landscapes of stately homes. As part of its range of garden ornaments Doulton produced statues (about 39 in. (1 m) tall) made of plain or glazed terracotta, employing leading artists to model them. The statues were initially based on classical figures but by the 1920s Doulton was producing whimsical figures of pixies or of children cuddling pets. Perhaps because of the rather sentimental nature of much early 20th century garden statuary, relatively few contemporary artists produce figurative ceramics for gardens. Artists and potters have shown much more interest in abstract sculpture (see Chapter 10).

The Victorians also had many kinds of garden pots. Decorated pots would be placed on terraces or at the side of lawns as ornaments, while plain flower pots were used for growing tender plants in greenhouses when it was cold. The pots would then be moved into the garden for the summer. Flower pot makers enjoyed a boom in the Victorian and Edwardian period as gardening became even more popular and plant nurseries opened to satisfy the demand for new plants.

The First World War changed everything. Royal and aristocratic families were deposed or made bankrupt and their gardens disappeared or atrophied. The social changes brought about by the war led to a decline in domestic servants and gardeners. This trend continued and after the Second World War very few British households had any servants or gardeners. Furthermore, by the 1950s, the mass production of cheap plastic pots meant that few country potteries in Britain were still in business as they were unable to compete.

Great gardens survived only as museums. The future of large gardens lay in municipal parks, and local councils soon became the biggest employers of gardeners. Homeowners them-

The use of a boulder with gravel and alpine plants reflects a Japanese influence in the design of Mr. and Mrs. Glazier's garden in Sheffield.

selves began to do their own gardening. Today designing for the small suburban garden is a booming business.

Television programs about gardening have introduced new and different design ideas for small gardens, such as Japanese styles or Mediterranean patios. These new garden designs have stimulated a demand for interesting pots and garden ornaments. This has coincided with a great expansion of ideas and creativity on the part of potters and artists in clay, who have been quick to perceive a new role for their work.

In the 1950s and 1960s many potters in Britain were influenced by Bernard Leach and Michael Cardew, so the emphasis was on functional pottery, particularly thrown tableware. Making plant pots was very much a marginal activity for artist potters. In the early 1970s exhibitions of work by

Hans Coper and Lucie Rie and the Americans Paul Soldner and Peter Voulkos had a profound effect on British ceramics. Their treatment of pots as sculptural forms was a revelation to students of ceramics at the time and encouraged many of them to experiment with new ways of working. Now, in the 1990s, along with handsome thrown pots, there are all kinds of interesting hand-built planters, decorative birdbaths, lanterns and ornamental features. A huge pot may have a role as a sculptural ornament while a small pot may serve as a plant container. Ceramic sculpture has moved outdoors.

In this book I shall look at the wide range and variety of outdoor ceramics, from thrown pots in Chapters 1 and 2, garden ornaments in Chapters 4, 5 and 6, to sculpture in Chapters 9 and 10. Many different techniques are used by makers of ceramics for open-air settings, but the image most associated with garden ceramics is that of the thrown plant pot and it is with this that I shall begin.

CHAPTER 1

THROWN POTS

The potter's wheel has been used for centuries to produce flower pots and those made in terracotta were the cheapest and most practical containers for plants. Their position was unchallenged until the 20th century when the production of cheap plastic pots threatened their survival.

Many artist potters are involved with the technique of throwing, and a number of them make pots specifically for gardens. While some of these throwers are motivated by a love of plants and gardens, others simply enjoy making big pots. There is little demand for large domestic pots these days as the invention of canning and the refrigerator have made large pots for the storing of food, wine or oil redundant. Gardens, however, provide a place for large, thrown pots.

Today there is an increasing demand for quality plant containers and ornamental pots, and garden designers and architects frequently seek out work from skilled artist potters. Many potters are keen to work on these projects. For some of the potters discussed in this chapter working on such commissions enables them to develop new ideas. They are interested both in making useful pots which integrate with people's lives and surroundings and in seeking new ways of working. Their work is varied in character and may suit an urban environment as much as a rural setting.

MARK PEDRO DE LA TORRE (UK)

De la Torre is inspired by a love of plants rather than by traditional flower pots. He makes tire-shaped terracotta pots in three or four sizes with a range of different surface treatments. These pots are all thrown and turned before he decorates them with patterned textures based on plant structure or foliage. The pots all have a similar form, but some are deeper than others to accommodate different sized plant roots. Various zigzag patterns which resemble the foliage of the house leek or sempervivum are used to decorate pots intended for succulents, cacti or low alpine plants. The pot and the plant are meant to be seen as a single entity and de la Torre feels that the pot is incomplete without its plant. Though his pots are a generous size they can be accommodated on a shelf or window sill. All are thrown in one piece and can be lifted easily.

Techniques

The clay body is a sanded red earthenware clay which is fired in an electric kiln to 2120°F (1160°C). The oxidizing atmosphere of the electric kiln produces a clean, bright red color in the clay. To guard against frost damage the pots are fired as close to vitrification as possible but not so that they lose the porosity which is important for plant welfare.

Working to commission is often a source of new ideas. Usually the client has a particular plant in mind so de la Torre gathers information about the plant's requirements, such as support and root depth, and then experiments with the form of the pot. He feels that his work develops slowly through a process of evolution.

A group of planters for alpines and succulents by Mark de la Torre.

ROB SLINGSBY (AUSTRALIA)

Rob Slingsby makes urns, flower pots, birdbaths, fountains and large individual jars. He enjoys the challenge of making really big pieces on the wheel and has specialized in making very large pots. Much of his work is commissioned for public spaces or particular projects. While many commissions are for big planters or jars, he has taken commissions from restaurants for clay ovens and has designed a highly efficient wood-fired oven. When time allows he collaborates with his wife, Shaunagh Willman, making a range of majolica baking dishes and tableware.

Slingsby believes it is important to establish integrity as a maker before undertaking large commissions in which many practical and aesthetic factors have to be considered. For the commission to succeed, the maker and the customer must each feel confident that their expectations will be met. Slingsby feels strongly that architects and designers who commission large-scale work should include the potter in the initial design process, as too often the potter is seen simply as a maker and brought in at a late stage when important decisions have already been made.

Techniques

Slingsby makes his pots by the coil-and-throw method but very large pieces often consist of several thrown pieces joined together. He uses a high-firing earthenware clay and decorates the pots with textures such as sprigs or pressed rope marks. The pots are finished with a non-porous terra sigillata slip made from the clay that he uses for throwing and it is applied to the dry pots by painting, spraying or dipping. The terra sigillata forms a thin coat which retains its sheen at any temperature and the work is fired to 2012°F (1100°C) in a 110 cu. ft. (3 m³) gas-fired trolley kiln.

Rob Slingsby working in his studio with large pots drying in the foreground.

CAMERON WILLIAMS (AUSTRALIA)

Cameron Williams is a thrower who specializes in making big pots. When he was younger he wanted a career which was both physically and artistically challenging and which would fit within a self-employed lifestyle – pottery seemed the natural choice. Williams makes functional pots which range from small-scale tableware to very large planters or fountains. He most enjoys making garden pieces because of the scale of the work involved. He likes his work to have a function, so even his sculptural pieces have a use, serving as fountains, lights or bird feeders. The garden

Cameron Williams standing next to one of his large jars.

Cameron Williams throwing the base ring of a large pot.

Williams and an assistant carrying a second stage ring with a grooved rim on its batt ready to fit over a base ring.

The second stage is placed on the base ring.

planters are shaped according to the needs of particular plants. Some plants require wide, shallow root space, others good drainage, and some like plenty of moisture.

Williams loves the wheel and tries to spend as much time as possible throwing. He uses terracotta clay and aims to make large, clean forms. Some of these may have sculptural additions that give them humor and movement. The pots are finished with either terra sigillata or vitreous slips and fired once. This avoids the problems of handling them a second time for glazing.

Techniques

His pots are thrown in stages and built up from wide, thrown rings of clay. The rim of the second stage ring is grooved so that it fits over the rim of

After removing the batt, Williams throws and smooths the two sections together.

Cleaning and smoothing the outside of the pot with the back of a flexible saw blade.

the lower section. The sections are joined and thrown and smoothed with a metal shim. More sections are added until the pot is the right size and shape. Williams has a small crane rig in the workshop for moving very large pots from the wheel to the drying area and the kiln trolley.

Other people share the workshop, so they help move big pots using slings, rollers, ramps and ropes.

Cameron Williams blends his own clay and fires his pots to 2012°F (1100°C) in a 300 cu. ft. (8.5 m³) gas-fired trolley kiln. The kiln is fired very slowly and pots near the burner ports are protected from direct flame by placing a shield of kiln bricks around them.

The finished pot is lifted away from the wheelhead by means of a hoist.

JOHN CLIFF (AUSTRALIA)

John Cliff makes a variety of work which includes large thrown planters as well as majolica-decorated thrown pots, many influenced by 16th century Italian *istoriato* pieces. His work is exhibited regularly in Sydney galleries. He makes other work to commission, such as decorative wall pieces for courtyards. These are often constructed of mosaic, sometimes combined with handpainted tiles, thrown vessels or press-molded forms.

Over the last few years Cliff has been involved with public art commissions. After an earthquake

Shallow bowl with majolica and luster decoration by John Cliff. Earthenware 2012°F (1100°C). D. 17.5 in. (45 cm).

in 1989 which devastated Hamilton, a suburb of the town of Newcastle, he was asked to undertake commissions relating to the rebuilding of Hamilton. This appealed to him, as he believes that art is a part of life rather than a separate entity residing in galleries and museums.

For the commission Cliff had to develop new techniques to address the technical problems arising from the sheer size of the pieces. One commission for pots for the Newcastle Workers' Club led him to collaborate with Cameron Williams, a specialist thrower (see below). The other commission was for large permanent planters for the main shopping street in Hamilton. For this, Cliff used mural-making techniques which are described in Chapter 8.

A Collaborative Commission – John Cliff and Cameron Williams

The design brief for the Newcastle Workers' Club was to supply 12 large decorative plant pots. The theme was to be aspects of the region and Cliff chose to look at the role of the Workers' Club, which was originally a recreational facility for trade union members. The design of the new club building made use of classical geometry and space, so Cliff based the planters on classical Greek forms. The pots were made of terracotta and decorated with colored slips.

To carry out the commission, Cliff worked in Williams' studio. The pots were designed by Cliff and thrown by Williams in two sections, base and body. Cliff decorated them using colored vitreous slips and terra sigillata. Each piece took approximately 220 lb. (100 kg) of clay to make. The clay was terracotta and the planters were fired on their rims in a gas-fired, fiber-lined 400 cu. ft. (11 m³) top-hat kiln to approximately 2012°F (1100°C).

LEFT: Plant pot on the theme of beaches made for the Newcastle Workers' Club, designed and decorated by John Cliff and thrown by Cameron Williams. H. 39 in. (1 m); W. 35 in. (90 cm).

RIGHT: Jardinière by Will Levi Marshall. Oxidized stoneware, 2336°F (1280°C) with additional lusters. H. 35 in. (90 cm); D. 12 in. (30 cm).

WILL LEVI MARSHALL (UK)

Marshall makes a range of functional pots which includes large jardinières and stools for the garden. Most of his work is thrown using a smooth textured stoneware clay body.

While he was in the USA studying for his MA he developed a strong interest in color and the way in which it can emphasize or enhance the forms of his work. As a result of his research into glazes Marshall has developed a range of stoneware glazes in bright vibrant colors which he applies in bold geometric shapes and curves on his pots. The work is fired to 2336°F (1280°C), and additional colors and metallic effects are produced by lusters applied after the glaze firing then re-fired to 1382°F (750°C).

SIMON HULBERT (UK)

Simon Hulbert's interest in garden pots began with research for his MA degree. He studied classical Greek architecture and the persistence of Western classicism in gardens and looked at this influence on English formal gardens of the 18th and 19th centuries. The use of ornament in formal and informal settings is the underlying element in his work and, while his pots may be plant containers, they are intended to function as a focal point or ornament in a particular garden design or location.

Hulbert set up his first studio in South Wales with the aid of a marketing initiative grant. He began by making a production line of terracotta ware, mainly plant pots, in a traditional English style. After six years in south Wales he spent two years in the Pacific, with seven months in Fiji where he worked on a pottery development project. He learned a lot from the village potters in Fiji and this has influenced his work. His pots now have softer and more varied shapes, while still remaining rooted in the English classical tradition.

Techniques

Hulbert uses red terracotta clay and his work ranges from plant pots to large monumental pieces. His techniques are a hybrid of handbuilding and throwing. Coiling, press-molding and throwing are all used in constructing his pieces. His smaller pots are mainly thrown while the large one-off pieces take many days to build by coiling. He seeks to maintain a classical sense of proportion in his forms while using a free approach which exploits the soft qualities of clay.

The pots are fired in a 60 cu. ft. (1.7 m³) gas kiln which allows him to make pieces up to 58.5 in. (1.5 m) in height. The firing temperature is high for red clay, in order to bring out colors and render the clay frostproof. Recently Hulbert has experimented with raw glazes and reactive slips which influence the texture of the glaze as well as the color. His largest pieces are usually made to commission and he sells his regular work from his own gallery in Hay-on-Wye. He is adaptable in his approach, and, while his thrown work has a close relationship with traditional terracotta forms, he uses handbuilding techniques, where appropriate, for individual pieces of a less symmetrical character.

Thrown urn by Simon Hulbert. H. 31 in. (80 cm); W. 9 in. (24 cm).

CHAPTER 2

THE NEW
COUNTRY POTTERS

Potters are currently making pots for the open air, using a wide varriety of methods, but there are some who value the sense of continuing a tradition and have chosen to become throwers. The adherence to an ideal of traditional thrown country pottery is particularly marked in Britain where the influence of Bernard Leach has been strongest. All the potters discussed in this chapter are British and live in the countryside. Many of them are graduates of university or art college, and a number of them learned their craft at one of the last surviving English country potteries – Wrecclesham in Surrey. Although most of them are working in terracotta rather than stoneware, many of them fire their work with wood. Some have views similar to those held by Bernard Leach, who shared the belief of the Arts and Crafts Movement that mechanization and urbanization had resulted in a degree of spiritual deprivation in society. Leach saw the production of pots by hand as a means of restoring traditional cultural values.

The appreciation of traditional garden pots is not confined to potters. It is shared by many keen garden owners who are now much more aware of design and are often interested in the pots as well as the plants. Today there is a healthy demand for good hand-thrown pots and people such as Jim Keeling and John Huggins have successfully moved into this new market for quality garden pots, setting up production potteries. Whether they work as individuals or run small production potteries, these potters continue to make and develop pots based on traditional styles. They could be regarded as the new generation of country potters.

When these potters make pots needing more than a single weight of clay they use two main methods. The first is to add successive thrown sections as described in the preceding chapter (see Cameron Williams' entry), and the second is to build up the pot with coils which are then smoothed and thrown into shape.

JIM KEELING AND WHICHFORD POTTERY (UK)

Jim Keeling studied history and archaeology at Cambridge University, but then decided he wanted to learn to throw pots. He became an apprentice at Wrecclesham Pottery, and the two elderly potters who worked there taught him how to throw large pots and to choose a good clay body. Clay had to be selected carefully because some red clays are suitable only for making small pots, and not all will resist frost after firing.

When Keeling set up Whichford Pottery in a Warwickshire village he did not want to be a solo artist potter, but part of a team. It gives him great satisfaction that Whichford Pottery now employs about 20 local people. The pottery started with a traditional range of thrown pots which were

Whichford Pottery on display at Waterperry House garden center, near Oxford.

based on the sizing scheme of the old country potters. This scheme worked on the system of the number of pots which could be made from a half hundredweight of clay (56 lb. or 25 kg). A Number 1 would be a single pot of the full weight, about 21 in. (53 cm) across; Number 2 would be half the weight of a Number 1, about 18 in. (45 cm) across. Number 60 would be a small pot about 3.5 in. (9 cm) in diameter. This range of pots is still produced at Whichford, and is now supplemented by a variety of other shapes and styles.

In 1985 Jim Keeling was awarded a Churchill Fellowship to study terracotta manufacturers abroad and he visited traditional potteries in Italy and Crete. On his return he introduced a range of hand-pressed pots to Whichford, based on those he saw in Italy. The method of hand-pressing clay into molds dates back to Roman times. It allows the production of square or oblong boxes and troughs, even of animals. The larger pots are decorated with swags of fruit, basket trellis, running leaf patterns or simply 'pastry' twists. Whichford has successfully combined these classical Mediterranean motifs with simple English country flower pots to produce a range of work which fits harmoniously into present day garden settings.

Techniques

Where possible the working methods at Whichford are traditional, but modern machinery is used where it saves on time-consuming drudgery. The pottery uses its own clay body made from a mixture of two local clays. The freshly dug clay is mixed to a slip in a blunger and passed through a sieve to remove impurities. Then the water is squeezed out in a filter press, a process which takes several hours, and a pugmill is used to complete the mixing of the clay. It is then left to age for several weeks before being used.

Jim Keeling's throwing techniques are based on the system he learned as an apprentice at Wrecclesham. He is capable of throwing big pots from a single weight of clay, but he makes larger ones from two thrown sections which are joined and then thrown again to attain the desired shape.

Whichford is a purpose-built pottery, so the kiln was constructed from scratch using modern materials such as ceramic fiber, which is an excellent insulator. Keeling and his team designed and built the kiln and have virtually dispensed with bricks in its construction. Fiber kilns permit very fast firing times so careful control is necessary to fire and cool the pots slowly. The top temperature is critical as the clay must be fully matured to ensure that the pots are frostproof. Over-firing would cause dramatic shrinkage and slumping of the form.

Hand pressed pedestal urn in Ham House style with a design of swags. By Whichford Pottery.
Photo: Robin Parrish.

JOHN HUGGINS (UK)

John Huggins has also set up a pottery which produces traditional style garden pots using locally dug clays. He too employs assistants and uses machinery, including a filter press and pugmill, to prepare the clay.

In his book *Pots for Plants and Gardens*, John Huggins stresses the importance of the right kind of clay. Not only do the pots have to be weather-

Terracotta pots by John Huggins.

proof and durable, but the clay must be highly plastic for large-scale throwing. The clays used by the industrial potteries around Stoke-on-Trent are too stiff and adding water to soften them only makes the clay sag. In his book, Huggins provides useful information on choosing a suitable plastic clay and preparing it for use by adding a temper such as sand.

Huggins' pots are decorated with traditional motifs but are not Italianate in style like the Whichford pots. He restricts himself to the use of simple roulette designs and sprigs. Most of his pots have a sturdy fat rim and the decoration is usually applied in a horizontal band below the rim.

Techniques

Huggins throws garden pots ranging from small sizes to very large ones requiring 45 lb. (20 kg) of clay. He does not attempt to put a whole 45 lb. lump of clay on the wheelhead all at once. Instead he builds up a cone of clay from three weighed lumps, which he puts on to the wheelhead one on top of the other. He beats the lumps together with his hands while the wheel is turning slowly so as to create a solid cone and center the clay as much as possible. Then the whole cone is lubricated with water and centered finally with the wheel spinning faster. Huggins uses his body weight to ease the clay to the center. He makes his biggest pots in two sections like Cameron Williams or Jim Keeling, and the sections are joined by pinching the rims together on the outside and the inside. The join is then beaten with a paddle before the pot is thrown and smoothed into its final shape.

Diagram showing how John Huggins builds up a cone of clay for throwing a large pot.

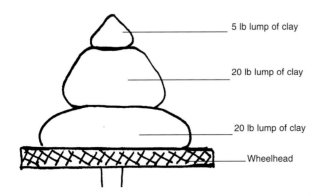

5 lb lump of clay

20 lb lump of clay

20 lb lump of clay

Wheelhead

MARK GRIFFITHS (UK)

Mark Griffiths learned to make pots through several apprenticeships during the 1970s. He first worked with a German potter, Fritz Stella, followed by a period with Colin Carr in Derbyshire. The most influential time was his three years working with Russell Collins at Hook Norton Pottery in Oxfordshire. He has always enjoyed throwing large pots so it seemed logical to him to make garden pots.

Techniques

Griffiths uses Ruabon tile clay which he buys ready pugged from the factory. He mixes the fresh clay in a dough mixer to attain the consistency he needs for throwing and the clay is stored for ageing for as long as possible before he has to use it. With this particular clay, he knows that if a finished pot absorbs less than 8% of its weight in water content it will be frostproof. To test this he weighs the fired pot while it is dry and then soaks it in water for a couple of days. He weighs the soaked pot and the difference between the two weights of the pot is the amount of water absorbed.

He usually makes big garden pots from thrown sections and may add as many as four sections, but he never adds more than the weight of the previous section. Adding less weight each time gives better control over the form, since any fault in the base section tends to become exaggerated as the pot grows. Griffiths often coils the rim and throws it into shape.

For pots with a diameter greater than 28 in. (70 cm), he adds coils to a stiffened thrown base and throws the coiled section into shapes. The coils are extruded through a multi-die on the pugmill. He sometimes uses a gas burner to speed the process of stiffening a thrown base section.

While Griffiths can lift a base section of a partly made pot on his own, lifting a finished pot requires two people. He has a hydraulic forklift to move very big pots around the studio. The tines of the fork fit under the batt on which the pot has been made and the whole assembly is lowered from the wheel on to two bricks on the floor of the studio.

Group of garden pots by Mark Griffiths.
Photo: Mark Griffiths.

As he does not have sufficient space to allow several large pots to dry slowly at the same time, Griffiths has made a drying unit. This is a 140 x 140 in. (3.6 x 3.6 m) insulated box with a dehumidifier and heat exchanger. It is capable of drying pots very quickly without damage, thus ensuring a good supply of dried work ready for firing. Large numbers of small pots can be accommodated in the unit on shelving, while a single big pot can be wheeled in. Drying takes about 48 hours. The kiln is a truck kiln designed to use with a forklift. He designed the arrangement himself after seeing a similar system in operation at Monica Young's pottery. Griffiths' work is fired to 1976°F (1080°C).

He makes a small range of standard garden pots and prefers to make pots to commission. He is now also making high-fired stoneware pots which are wood- or salt-fired, but most of his output is pots for gardens. He feels that, as a maker of garden pots, he is making a contribution to a garden design with the pot, while the purchaser decides on its location and chooses the plants.

MICK PINNER (UK)

Although Mick Pinner's work has its roots in the English country pottery tradition, he has moved away from the classical garden pot imagery which Huggins and Keeling use in their work. The majority of his garden planters are thrown urns and tubs made from a local red clay, and salt-fired to give subtle color variations and occasional 'flash' marks on the surface. Rather than being the traditional terracotta red, colors range from soft pinks to greys and blacks produced by the flame and salt in the kiln.

Pinner studied ceramics at Farnham School of Art and then worked as an assistant at Wrecclesham Pottery for two years. He now has his own pottery in Hampshire. Pinner's skill in throwing very large pots has put him in an ideal position to accept major commissions, such as making pots for National Trust houses like Ham House in London.

Pinner not only makes garden pots but also large individual pieces inspired by medieval English pots or Japanese stoneware jars, particularly those of Tamba and Shigaraki. He makes forms that interest him and leaves it to the customer to decide what use they can make of them. His jars can function as planters although sometimes people leave them empty and use them as garden features or place them indoors in a sitting room or hall.

Pinner is interested in geology and the weathering of rocks and he visualizes the making of pots as almost a geological process itself because soft mud-like clay is compressed when the pot is formed, then heated in the kiln to produce a rock-like substance. This is similar to mud

Garden pots by Mick Pinner standing on their rims to dry out.

29

sediments which were compressed over time before drying out and being subjected to volcanic heat which transformed them into different kinds of rock. This process is echoed in the surface qualities of Pinner's pots. He throws with very soft clay which shows the pressure marks of his tools. Although the fired pot is hard, it still looks soft and freshly made.

Techniques

Pinner has three wheels – an industrial double-cone wheel, a continental kick wheel and a geared kick wheel, and he throws pots up to about 45 lb. (20 kg) in weight from one piece of clay. For making larger pots he adds coils to a thrown base section. Pinner mainly uses a Sussex red brick clay which he buys 'as dug' and then prepares at the workshop.

As Pinner throws he forms the shape of the pot by pressure from the inside and he uses wood and metal ribs to control and compress the clay.

Jar form by Mick Pinner showing pink, grey and black marks produced during the firing. H. 16 in. (40 cm).

The ribs press over a larger area of clay than fingertips alone, thus avoiding weakening the clay walls at localized pressure points. They leave marks which the potter feels enhance his forms. He turns very little, only trimming away enough clay to make a foot for the pot without losing its thrown character.

His kiln, designed specifically for firing large terracotta pots, is oil-fired and of a circular down-draught design. This is a large kiln of 180 cu. ft. (5 m³) which he fills and fires about ten times a year. Pinner normally fires his pots for 50 hours to 2102°F (1150°C), the upper end of the firing range of his clay body. He rarely uses glazes, preferring a type of salt firing instead. Small containers of salt are positioned among the pots to be fired, some of which have a coat of slip. The salt vapor is carried on to the pots during firing, thus causing localized glazing and flashing. The reduction firing and the salt create a tougher than normal finish which protects the pots against frost damage.

Since some of the large pots are too heavy to lift, Pinner slides them around on boards. He uses pieces of foam rubber or straw bales as a support for tipping a big pot of 100–200 lb. (45–91 kg) upside down to work on the base.

JONATHAN GARRATT (UK)

Jonathan Garratt's work represents a different aspect of English country pottery tradition. While throwing is at the center of his work, he is consciously trying to develop new planter forms rather than continuing with traditional flower pot shapes. He makes terracotta pots in a wide range of designs for patios, conservatories and gardens. Garratt feels that bright orange terracotta can dominate the plants, so his pots come in soft, dusky tones of wine-red and browns produced by wood-firing. He is a keen plantsman and he prefers these quieter hues so that the pots fit comfortably into planting schemes.

Garratt has a pottery in a small Dorset village and lives the life of a country potter. He discovered pottery at Eton School where he was taught

Wall planter in a soft brown color by Jonathan Garratt.

Chinese style tripod pot by Jonathan Garratt.

by Gordon Baldwin. He continued his interest in pottery while at Cambridge and, after graduating, decided to become a potter. He worked in rural potteries for a couple of years before going to Nigeria to work as an assistant to Michael O'Brien, who had succeeded Michael Cardew at Abuja pottery.

Garratt draws on many sources of inspiration, including pottery from China and Nigeria. This is reflected in his wide and varied range of work which includes many types of planters, wall pots, nest pots for small birds, jars and tripod shaped flower pot holders based on Chinese pots. He decorates the pots with geometric patterns based on

West African textile designs, using homemade roulettes and stamps.

Techniques

Garratt refines his own clay at the pottery. This means he can produce a tough clay body which can withstand frost. The clay is dug from a local pig farm, blunged to a slip and then passed through a sieve to remove stones and roots before being left to dry in a settling tank. When

The outside of Garratt's circular down-draught kiln with pots drying in the warmth.

Clay in Garratt's settling tank cut into blocks ready for pugging.

Jonathan Garratt throwing.

View of pots packed into the chamber of Garratt's kiln.

the clay is stiff but not yet dry it is cut into blocks and pugged. The clay is stored for several months before it is used. His local clay has a fine silt content so he adds two grades of sand to achieve a suitable matrix of different size particles for ease of throwing and to improve frostproofing. Ball clay is added for strength. The clay is put through the pugmill twice before it is ready for throwing.

Garratt has two wheels, one electric and the other a large continental kick wheel.

The kiln is a round down-draught kiln of 250 cu. ft. (7 m³) capacity with a 270 in. (7 m) chimney. The firing chamber is 81 in. (2.1 m) high by 81 in. (2.1 m) in diameter. Garratt can fill the kiln with pots made from 2460 lb. of plastic clay. Every six weeks the kiln is fired, entirely with wood, to 2012°F (1100°C). It takes three days to pack, 17 hours to fire and four days to cool. Wood consumption is about 3920 lb. per firing.

CLIVE BOWEN (UK)

Clive Bowen came to pottery after studying painting at Cardiff School of Art. He found it difficult to interest art galleries in his paintings and found the attitude of many of them discouraging. Convinced that there would be no easy entry into the art world, but wishing to do something creative, he decided to train as a potter. To some extent this was a lifestyle choice. It was the 1960s and Bowen was very influenced by the music and films of that period.

He became an apprentice to Michael Leach after marrying his daughter and then worked as a production potter at Brannam's Pottery in Barnstaple. He was influenced by the Leaches, but it was Michael Cardew who inspired him to fire pots with wood.

Bowen is very aware of the traditions of Devon country pottery and has consciously tried to work within that tradition without copying Devon pots. He admires European slipware and Oriental pots, particularly those of Korea and Japan, and for many years he made domestic pots in slip-decorated earthenware. He likes the effects of vapor and flame when firing with wood, and he became noted for the fresh, painterly way he used slip decoration which contrasted with the dark, reduction-fired background color of the clay.

Bowen has succeeded in making a living as a full-time potter but this has meant that market forces have had an effect on the type of pots he

Group of unglazed garden planters by Clive Bowen.

produces. He began making garden pots after being commissioned by two National Trust houses in Devon. As the demand for large garden pots has increased in recent years and Bowen enjoys working on a bigger scale, he now also makes very large jars. His garden pots are often unglazed and have a pale, natural buff color.

Techniques

Bowen attaches great importance to the rhythm of repetition throwing, wherein the process becomes almost as unconscious and natural as walking. He feels that his best work is made during this natural flow, rather than when too much thinking is involved. This natural knowledge of throwing only comes after years of regular, intensive practice.

Clive Bowen throwing.
Photo: Keith Duncan.

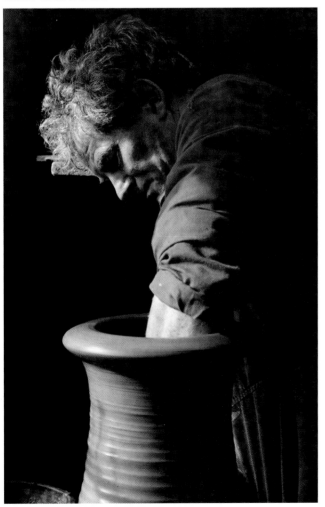

He uses red clay from Fremington in Devon where he lives and works. All his work is thrown. Like Jonathan Garratt, he has a large wood-firing kiln of a circular design based on Michael Cardew's kiln. It is approximately 93 in. (2.4 m) in diameter and is high enough for him to stand up in. The clay for the white and yellow slips comes from a nearby village and clay for red slip comes from the stream at the bottom of his garden.

Slip-decorated garden pot by Clive Bowen.

SVEND BAYER (UK)

Svend Bayer lives and works in the same Devon village as Clive Bowen. He has a large, wood-fueled kiln and he fires his work to high stoneware temperatures. His garden pots are part of a wide range of thrown domestic pots. He uses glazes sparingly, mainly for the insides of functional items such as jugs. The outside of a pot is glazed only by the flying ash produced in the wood-fired kiln. At high stoneware temperature, the ash reacts with the surface of the clay to form a glaze. The result is natural variations in color and surface texture, produced by the movement of the flames inside the kiln.

Techniques

Bayer makes his big pots through a combination of throwing and coiling. He starts the pot with a thrown base, but does not try to center a solid mass of clay. Instead he works with the wheel turning slowly and uses his fist to beat the lump of clay into a pad for the pot base and he forms a ring to make the sides. Once he is satisfied that the base ring is as regular as possible, he wets it with water, speeds up the wheel, centers it and throws the pot in the normal manner. Bayer then builds up the pot from carefully weighed coils which he smooths on and paddles with a wooden tool before continuing to throw. The whole pot is constructed of successive coils and the shape is controlled by paddling as well as throwing. The sturdy rim is made from a coil which is smoothed but not thinned by the throwing process.

Wood-fired garden pots by Svend Bayer on display at The Harley Gallery, Nottinghamshire.
Photo: Robin Parrish.

CHRIS LEWIS (UK)

Chris Lewis makes thrown stoneware pots in a full range of sizes and types, including tableware, and garden pots up to 58 in. (1.5 m) in height. He also makes handbuilt stoneware garden seats, pillars, birdbaths, water features and sculptural pieces. He likes his work to be of sufficient size to have an impact in an outdoor setting.

He learned to throw at Wrecclesham Pottery in 1975. It was there he discovered that the only restrictions on the size of a pot were throwing skill and the size of the kiln. He then spent a period of time traveling in West Africa and, after returning to England, he worked with the potter Ursula Mommens in Sussex. Lewis remained in Sussex, establishing his own pottery business and eventually he built his own large wood-fueled kiln. At the time he thought the kiln was of sufficient size to take the biggest pots he would ever make. He soon found that it was not large enough.

Lewis does not apply glaze to his garden pots but, as they are fired in a wood kiln, they become thinly glazed with fly ash.

Wood-fired jar by Chris Lewis.

ANDREW MCGARVA (UK/FRANCE)

Although Andrew McGarva now lives and works in France, his work is rooted in English traditional pottery. He likes to make usable pots, whether they are for the table, for cooking or for growing plants. When he was a student he often visited Wrecclesham Pottery where flower pots were being made. He also had a period working in La Borne in France, a pottery village which used to make large crocks for salting meat.

When McGarva was working in England he started by making stoneware flower pots, but he changed to working with red clay as he feels it ages better and is cheaper to fire than stoneware. Its porosity is also better for the health of plants. Although he still makes garden pots, they have become something of a sideline as there is only a limited demand for them in his area of France.

He makes the plant pots in frostproof red clay, fired to a rich red color at about 1940°F (1060°C).

His garden pots have open forms with no constriction at the shoulder, thus ensuring that soil can expand freely if it freezes without cracking the pot. The pots are decorated with home-made clay stamps. Some are decorated with slip and a galena (lead ore) glaze but these pots are not frostproof.

Techniques

Andrew McGarva's pottery is located at an old tile works. He digs his own clay from a field nearby. The clay is then blunged down in a dough mixer, sieved and run out into drying pans. When it is right for throwing, it is bagged up and left in the store for a year to age. When ready, the clay is pugged once before being shaped into balls and thrown on a motorized momentum wheel.

McGarva's largest plant pots are made in two sections. He rarely makes any that are heavier than 75 lb. (35 kg), a size he can still manipulate and fire rim to rim with another pot in the kiln.

Up until now the pots have been fired in a gas-fueled kiln, but McGarva plans to start wood-firing some of his work.

The potters featured in these two chapters are all men. There are many women potters who throw but, during my research for this book, I found that those potters who are drawn to throwing very big pots are almost exclusively men. Many women potters work on a large scale but I discovered none who are throwers. Physical strength as well as skill is required to throw heavy weights of clay and so women who make big work have chosen other methods.

However, I believe that there are other reasons why it is mostly men who are involved with throwing large pots. These men are attracted by the technique itself and by the challenges of throwing such big sizes, or of firing traditional kilns.

The potters in the next chapter have very varied approaches to making plant containers. Many of these potters are women.

Red clay plant pot by Andrew McGarva.

CHAPTER 3

HANDBUILT POTS AND PLANTERS

While throwing makes physical demands and places certain constraints on the shapes of pots, handbuilding techniques open up a different range of options. This has led potters such as Simon Hulbert and Andrea Wulff to adopt handbuilding techniques for some of their work. Handbuilding techniques allow for the construction of large pieces and a variety of shapes which could not be achieved by throwing, and most of the potters discussed in this chapter never throw.

The production of handbuilt planters has burgeoned in the 1980s, though some potters such as

Peter Stoodley have been making handbuilt planters since the 1950s. His planters are made of stoneware and decorated with inlaid slips and applied relief and they are usually left unglazed. Stoodley's planter designs have a timeless quality and they have endured as classic pieces.

While the thrower aims to reproduce the same form in large numbers, the handbuilder works more slowly and aims to make planters which are also sculptural forms. The containers are intended to be complete forms in their own right but they should also complement the plants. For some makers such as Jane Norbury and Andrea Wulff the work must be seen with specific plants. Gordon Cooke goes a step further. For many of his pieces he conceives the pot and the plant as a single integrated form.

Coiled pot, 31 x 19.5 in. (80 x 50 cm), by Simon Hulbert.

Coiled stoneware pots with relief decoration by Peter Stoodley.

GORDON COOKE (UK)

Gordon Cooke does not use traditional shapes for his planters because he is interested in finding new associations between plant material and decorative forms and surfaces. He likes the contrast between the static, hard ceramic material and the growing, soft plant and he experiments with the relationships between textures and color. He believes this is an area that has not received enough attention from artists.

Although best known for his fine sculptural porcelain, Cooke started his career as a landscape designer and so as a potter, it seemed a natural step to make pots for the garden. The majority of his planters are made in stoneware but some small-scale porcelain pieces also contain plants. He matches the pots with appropriate plants and sells the complete piece with instructions for plant care. Cooke does not exhibit his garden ceramics in galleries because plant care can be a problem for gallery owners. Instead he sells the planters through exhibitions at his home where he has an interesting garden which he designed

Stoneware 'Pebble' with porcelain slips, oxides and ash glaze by Gordon Cooke.

himself. Customers respond to seeing his work in an accessible domestic setting.

Cooke takes inspiration from many sources. He is currently working on a series of ideas based on Japanese garden fences made from wicker and cane, while past sources have included mosaic floors and Moorish patterns. His work is varied because he likes to explore an idea in depth for a period of time before moving on to a new theme.

His plant pots are all small-scale and intended for use in a conservatory or on a patio, although he has made large ceramic structures for the garden (see Chapter 9). The work is fired to stoneware temperatures but Cooke advises his customers to protect their pots from frost as a precaution.

Techniques

His garden pots are all slab-built or press-molded from a grogged stoneware clay such as Craft Crank. He creates textures by using coils and 'scrapings', sometimes applying mixed clays and porcelain clay to the surface. Cooke finds the

character of unglazed Craft Crank unattractive, so porcelain slips and oxides are applied after bisque firing to 1832°F (1000°C). The slips are applied by brush or sponge to give some color and texture. He prefers decoration which does not rely on a glaze for its main effect, but he sometimes uses reduction-fired ash glazes made with ash from his open fire. These high-fired glazes produce subtle colors and surface effects. Cooke fires his planters in a Laser gas kiln to cone 8 (2305°F/1263°C) after bisque firing.

Stoneware planter with stoneware additions by Gordon Cooke. Bottle glass in top of columns. H. 9 in. (24 cm). F. & J. Davenport collection.

JANE NORBURY (UK/FRANCE)

Jane Norbury started making planters when she had a studio in London and worked on commissions from garden designers. These commissions were mainly for one-off pieces, but she soon discovered that there was a demand for unusual and individual plant containers.

Since she moved to France she has specialized in making planters along with lighting features, sconces, chandeliers and candlesticks. Her pottery studio in France – created in an old barn with a field behind – gives her the space to make and store large-scale work and the opportunity to create her own garden. She has developed a practical knowledge of plants and she experiments with different combinations of plants with pots. She seeks out plants that can be set off by a particular pot through color, form and scale but where neither the pot nor the plant dominates.

Her handbuilt terracotta planters are constructed from embossed slabs and painted with thin layers of colored slips. Pots may be designed for a particular plant or setting and Norbury often decorates her pots with a leaf motif.

Window box with scallop shell pattern by Jane Norbury.

Techniques

Norbury works with a tile clay from Provence to which she adds grog. She wedges in the grog by hand, a laborious process, but she likes the tile clay as it is very plastic. After rolling out slabs of clay she cuts them with wires so that the grog gives them a granular texture, then she stamps the slabs with plaster or metal dies, or presses them into plaster molds. On the following day the slabs are joined to form the pots. She has a variety of designs for feet and extruded rims which she adds to the planters. She only paints her work when it is completely dry as this gives her a better picture of the fired results. A thin layer of white slip is washed over the pots and thin layers of colored body stains are added; sometimes she rubs off some of the color to get the clay breaking through.

Except for pieces that are glazed on the inside, her work is fired once only, to 1904°F (1040°C) in a Laser gas kiln. The planters are heavy and, although the kiln is an accessible front loader, she has not yet resolved the problem of handling the largest pots. One of the reasons she chose her house in France

Plant pot with embossed leaf pattern by Jane Norbury.

was because the studio and the exhibition space were both on the ground floor with no steps to negotiate.

Her pots have survived several Burgundy winters where the temperature usually drops to 5°F (-15°C). The shape of most of her planters is conical. This allows room for the earth to expand upwards when it freezes and since the clay is heavily grogged it allows water to pass through more easily. The firing temperature is relatively high for terracotta (1904°F/1040°C) and this contributes to frost resistance as well. Although Norbury is careful about the way she makes her pots to ensure that they will withstand frost, she likes other effects of weathering which gives them an aged feel.

She sells her planters through plant or pot shops in France, Holland and Italy and she also participates in France's biggest flower show at Château Courson.

ANDREA WULFF (GERMANY)

Andrea Wulff also seeks a perfect union between the clay pot and the living plant and keeps the final setting of plant and pot very much in mind. She tries to give each ceramic piece a natural earthy form, be it a tiny bowl or a large vase. She uses the clay to create forms with a sense of growth and with strong surface texture.

Wulff has always felt drawn to working in clay and does not see much point in either lengthy analysis of motivation or definition of a philosophy. She likes working with her hands and planting the finished pots.

Wulff also makes kitchenware such as pepper grinders, bread bins and herb sprinklers, but she feels that garden ceramics are where she can fully realize her artistic and creative ideas.

When working on specific commissions Wulff visits the site and plans the pots accordingly. However, she often finds that clients place orders

Planter with relief and combed texture by Andrea Wulff. Green, brown and white slips.
Photo: Erika Urlesberger.

because they like the individual nature of her work, so they simply indicate the colors and size they would like and then leave the rest to her.

Techniques

Wulff's pots are either handbuilt or thrown. She uses heavily grogged clays which are suitable across a wide range of firings, though she is currently working at earthenware temperatures (1976°F/1080°C) using an electric top-loading kiln. All the color in the pots is produced from slips, oxides and the natural color in the clay. Glaze is only used when it is really necessary for waterproofing objects such as saucers or dishes for plant pots. This glaze is transparent so as not to lose the colors of the pot. Her pots are heavy but they are built in such a way that she can normally move them by herself.

Because of the open character of the clay body and the fact that it is not fully matured at the earthenware firing temperature, the pots are not frostproof. This does not worry Wulff as she feels that weathering enlivens and enriches the surface of the pots and contributes to their character. She regards it as a process of evolution in her work.

Pink earthenware plant container with relief decoration by Andrea Wulff.
Photo: Erika Urlesberger.

THOMAS GALE (USA)

Unlike Wulff, Thomas Gale actively seeks to avoid frost damage in his work. He is constantly looking for better ways of making his low-fired terra sigillata planters more frost resistant.

He makes large terracotta coiled and thrown planter forms with a fired terra sigillata surface. These are typically about 23 in. (60 cm) high and have an architectural quality to them. Some are mounted on stands.

He says he is not much of a gardener, as he was primarily interested in designing and making ceramics before becoming involved with plants. Nevertheless his plantings show a strong awareness of the relationship between the character of the plant and the form and texture of the pot. Gale finds that planters present an interesting set of design problems and he is intrigued with the aspects of combining artistic form with the functional needs of living plants.

When he lived in Arizona for a number of years he became frustrated with the lack of quality large-scale planters available. He noticed that there were very few good terracotta pots to fit the Santa Fe style of home with its patios, entryways and gardens based on Spanish and Mexican architecture. It was then that planter forms became his primary interest.

Gale began by making high temperature wood-fired planters with ash-glazed surfaces but now he does not have access to a wood kiln and so has developed a range of work in terracotta.

He studied under the Japanese potter Yukio Yamamoto, first at the University of Northern Arizona and later in Japan. On his return to the USA he realized that Japanese style pots would not make him a good living, so he started to look for a clear market niche. He then enrolled in a Master of Fine Arts program and studied

Triangular planter on three-legged stand by Tom Gale. Terracotta with black slip. 23 x 28 in. (58 x 72 cm).

Old mission in Southwestern USA showing Spanish style architecture.
Photo: Dr Dora Perry-Wilson.

Plant container with terra sigillata slip, 17 in. (43 cm), by Tom Gale.

sculpture under the late Larry Elsner. It was here that he began constructing large earthenware vessels which relate to the architectural styles of the Southwestern USA. He is developing an interest in architectural forms and intends to move towards combining planter forms with architectural elements.

Techniques

Gale starts his planter forms with a thrown section such as a bowl. He then moves the thrown form on to a turntable and builds on to it using three or four rows of coils at a time. He allows the lower walls to stiffen as he continues to build upwards. When the tops of the walls are sufficiently stiff, he finishes off the planter with a thrown rim. Most of the time he uses low-fire terracotta clay which he buys in dry form.

Once the finished planters are completely dry he bisques them to cone 04 (1922°F/1050°C) in oxidation. After the bisque firing he sprays terra sigillata on to the outer surface of the planter, polishes it to a shine and refires it to cone 010 (1634°F/890°C) in oxidation. When the planter has been fired and cooled he sprays and buffs the surface with an aerosol spray wax to seal and protect the finished surface. The combination of thrown and coiled methods allows him greater freedom in shaping the form.

Gale avoids having to do a lot of lifting by keeping his working areas at the same height and using trolleys or carts to move work around the studio. His methods are very similar to those described by Jenifer Jones and Jim Robison in 'Practical Considerations' on page 143.

KARIN HESSENBERG (UK)

Like some of the other potters in this book who went to art school in the early 1970s, I was imbued with the ideals of the studio potter. Throwing was central to my work and I became known for my burnished, sawdust-fired porcelain pots. About ten years ago I abandoned throwing in favor of handbuilding as I felt that the wheel was restricting my ideas. Coincidentally, other throwers from the same generation, such as Kate Mellors and Christine-Ann Richards, also started working on large-scale garden pots at about the same time. It seems to have been a subconscious response to an expansion of ideas and fresh attitudes to ceramics which occurred in Britain in the 1980s. The orthodoxy of the wheel as the centerpiece of studio pottery was being challenged.

In my own work questions about the purpose of my pots coincided with a developing interest in gardening and a desire to work on a large scale. I also wanted to see art playing a useful part in people's everyday lives rather than existing on the periphery in galleries.

Karin Hessenberg's three-tier planter in Kathmandu pattern. Stoneware with blue ash glaze. H. 21 in. (53 cm).

I was inspired by the elaborate patterned architecture I saw on visits to India and Nepal in the 1980s. This provided ideas for both the forms and patterns of many of my garden pots and I now make slab-built planters which range from small window boxes to large plant stands. I also make birdbaths and sundials and occasionally figurative sculptures for special orders.

Techniques

All my work is made from high-fired stoneware clay which is raw-glazed and fired to 2336°F (1280°C) in an electric kiln. Full details of my making methods are described in Chapter 5.

I try to ensure that my smaller planters are interesting forms in their own right, but keep them simple enough to complement the plants. The larger plant towers are designed to have a sculptural and decorative presence and they can be kept outdoors or placed in a conservatory. They are constructed in tiers to endow them with an architectural character, and I decorate them with patterned textures which are pressed into the soft clay with plaster stamps. Some of my planters are decorated only with sprig bosses and relief molded rims. I usually leave it to the purchaser to decide how they will plant the pots, though sometimes I will suggest plant arrangements that I think have been successful.

I make tall pieces such as plant towers and birdbaths from separate modules which fit together after firing. Usually there is a top section which fits into a pedestal. This method was dictated by the shape and size of my front-loading kiln, which only accommodates a single large pot or module, or several smaller pots. The maximum height I can fire is 23 in. (60 cm) and this also happens to be the biggest size I can lift by myself. I try to avoid making anything that I cannot lift. The most worrying time is loading a dry, raw-glazed piece into the kiln.

Pots intended to be kept outdoors have to withstand harsh weather and my work has stood up to the rigors of Scottish winters. This is because of the high firing temperature (2301–2336°F/1260–1280°C) and the glaze on the pots which prevents ice forming in the pores of the coarse-grained clay body. With items such as birdbaths which hold water permanently, I seal the finished basin by painting it with a liquid silicone water sealant as used in the building trade. It is colorless and eliminates any residual porosity caused by the open character of Craft Crank clay.

Cusco pattern plant tower by Karin Hessenberg. Stoneware with blue ash glaze. H. 22 in. (57 cm).

STEPHEN DIXON (UK)

Stephen Dixon's terracotta planters draw on a tradition of garden ornament known as 'rococo', with flutings, heads, foliage and fruit sprigs and bosses applied to the pots. Garden pots were initially a sideline which he started as a cheaper range of work to sell alongside his one-off studio pieces. They provided a useful income at the start of his pottery business.

He is best known for his narrative boxes covered with modeled figures which are often hybrids of humans and animals. These creatures carry weapons, dance, eat or drink from flagons. They may be accompanied by frolicking animals or clusters of fruit and flowers.

Dixon uses these figurative elements in much of his garden ceramics. His garden work has gradually become larger and more individual, and he makes wall planters and fountains which display his relish for decorative and sculptural details. Recently these garden pieces have developed into large-scale structures and murals. He is currently interested in recycling architectural materials, such as brick and stone and integrating these with contemporary tiles and images to make murals or freestanding constructions.

He has become involved with the restoration of ancient buildings and attempts to make site-specific work in sympathy with the environment. At the same time he aims to tell a story or provide an educational or historical viewpoint through the work.

Techniques

Dixon's work is principally terracotta. He uses a 50:50 mix of Vingerling Sculptors red clay and white St Thomas stoneware. He applies washes of color and glazes his work with a transparent lead glaze fired to 2138°F (1170°C) in an electric kiln. He enhances the details of the sculptures with bronze- and iron-like colors.

His main making methods are press molding and modeling. Some work, such as tiles, is made in white St Thomas stoneware clay. He constructs large-scale work from small, manageable units. The work is made weatherproof by the firing temperature (2138°F/1170°C) and by using heavily grogged clay.

Terracotta wall planters by Stephen Dixon.

ANTJE SCHARFE (GERMANY)

Antje Scharfe's handbuilt and constructed planters occupy a borderline position between architecture and garden ceramics. They were produced as part of a number of commissions she carried out in the 1980s. Garden ceramics are not typical of Scharfe's work and she only makes them to commission. She is best known for her work with fine bone china and porcelain.

Techniques

Her garden or architectural pieces are geometric forms with inlaid decoration. She uses a grogged stoneware body with inlaid porcelain and the planters or sculptural forms are partly glazed and fired to maturity, usually in oxidation in an elec-tric kiln. The firing temperature makes the work frostproof. Scharfe has devised her own methods of moving these heavy pieces using rollers and leverage where necessary.

As we have seen, large plant containers of all kinds have a decorative as well as a functional role to play in the open air setting, and many of the handbuilt planters in this chapter have been developed primarily as ornaments for a particular location. It is a logical step for pots to become ornaments in their own right and this is the subject of the next chapter.

Constructed architectural plant container by Antje Scharfe. Stoneware with inlaid porcelain.

CHAPTER 4

POTS AS
ORNAMENTS

The artists in this chapter make pots which are designed to create a focal point in a garden or landscape. Though many of the pots have modern forms, they are in a tradition developed from Roman and Mediterranean gardens where ornamental urns and vases were placed along avenues or on flights of steps. The best surviving example is the series of huge storage jars in the ancient Cretan palace at Knossos, and similar jars are still being made in Crete today.

In Spain the very large clay jars called *tinajas* are no longer used to store olive oil or wine, but they are often seen upright or on their sides decorating the forecourts of roadside restaurants. Both the Cretan jars and the Spanish *tinajas* are handbuilt by coiling. The large coil pots made by Jenifer Jones and Monica Young link in with this Mediterranean tradition.

All the potters whose work I describe in this chapter appreciate the sculptural qualities of pot forms. Some make rounded pots which are traditional in shape while others explore asymmetrical forms with fine textures or with crusted knobbly surfaces. Most of the potters handbuild with coils but a few combine handbuilding with throwing to construct their pots.

ABOVE: Group of *tinajas* in a garden in Elche, Spain. *Photo: Robin Parrish.*

BELOW: Installation of terracotta pots by Franz Stahler at The New Arts Centre, Roche Court, Wiltshire. This installation refers to traditional large Mediterranean store jars. H. 59 in. (1.52 m).

BILLY ADAMS (UK)

Adams' garden pots evolved from his more regular output after he placed some large pieces in the open and realized that his work would suit outdoor settings. Landscape is a source of inspiration for most of his work, and making pots for the open air was a natural progression. His vessel forms are designed to be focal points in a garden or landscape. He is particularly interested in the way in which man-made and natural structures interact in a landscape and his observations of rocks and sky inspire the textures and colors of his pots. He makes pots with decorative handles and twists, based on classical bowl or goblet forms. For Adams the challenge is to make work which has sufficient presence not to be dominated by the scale of the garden.

Techniques

Adams' pots are mainly handbuilt with some thrown elements. He usually starts his pots from a thrown base and then builds up in several stages using coils of three different sorts of clay. First there is an interior layer of coarse Craft Crank followed by a middle layer of mixed clay which prevents uneven shrinkage of the pot during firing. Finally he adds an outer skin of porcelain which is encouraged to buckle and crack as the inside of the pot is shaped. This gives the pot a fine, hard texture. At a later stage he introduces a contradictory form such as a circular thrown handle or a smooth rim, which is intended to symbolize the intervention of man in the natural world.

Although Adams works rapidly while building the pots, he works in stages to allow the clay to harden before adding more coils. It can take up to ten days to allow the pot to harden between stages of building.

After biscuit firing, the pot is given a base glaze high in china clay and fired to 2336°F (1280°C) to vitrify the clay and ensure that the many small surface fissures do not remain porous. Adams then adds more glazes which he fires successively at lower temperatures of 2012°F (1100°C) and 1832°F (1000°C). The different glazes combine to give rich greys, blues, reds and yellows.

Although his pots are large, Adams ensures that their size and weight are manageable enough for him to deliver and install himself. The high-firing temperature and the drainage holes in the pots ensure that they are frostproof.

Landscape planter by Billy Adams.

Elliptical vessel by Billy Adams.

JENIFER JONES (UK)

Although some of Jones' pieces have the size and scale of sculpture, they are pots and are conceived as such. She feels that pots have a character and associations distinct from those of a piece of sculpture and she thinks it is important that pot making should not lose its particular and separate identity. Her pots are not so much plant containers as ornamental elements in a garden design. Each pot is unique, with its own individual form and decoration.

Jones became interested in making pots for gardens when a friend asked her to make a large pot for her garden. The project opened up new possibilities as it brought together her growing interest in making large-scale pieces and her long-standing pleasure in gardens. At the time she was making small thrown or pinched pots in porcelain, but she also made the occasional large coiled piece in stoneware clay as a relief from the tension of handling fragile pieces. Now she has come to prefer making large pots as she feels at ease working on this scale. Each pot is substantial enough to relate to the human scale of a garden, while its form and decoration work well with the detail of the surrounding planting.

Coiled bottle form with incised decoration by Jenifer Jones. H. 20 in. (52 cm).

Jones finds it difficult to identify direct sources of inspiration but believes that certain things she has seen have provided an unconscious source of ideas. On a visit to Crete in the 1970s she was impressed by the huge pots in the ruins of the palace at Knossos and she was surprised to see similar recently made, modern pots (*pithoi*), in gardens and outside local houses there. It was a vision of pots as part of the landscape.

She admires Egyptian sculpture, particularly the monumental black basalt pieces, as well as unglazed pottery from Japan and Nigeria. However, she feels that her main interest is in the Mediterranean tradition.

Techniques

Jones builds her pots by coiling because she prefers this slow, concentrated method of

Tall handbuilt urn with incised geometric decoration by Jenifer Jones. H. 25 in. (64 cm).

working to throwing and likes the slight asymmetry that results from coiling. Though this asymmetry may be an almost imperceptible irregularity, she finds it important for the character of each pot. Coiling has also enabled her to work on a scale that would be far beyond her strength in throwing.

Jones uses a coarse-textured clay body based on Crank Mixture which is strong and robust and

Group of large coiled urns by Jenifer Jones in the South Courtyard, Queen Elizabeth II Conference Centre, London.

provides the rough texture and warm color that she likes. The clay is ordered in 2000 lb. (approx. 1 tonne) loads so that she can have the mixture made to her specification. She works on three or four pots at the same time, moving from one to the other as the clay dries. These pots will often be a related group based on a particular idea.

When the form of a pot is complete and the clay leatherhard, she incises or scores geometric patterns using a small knife. The pots are left to dry for three to four weeks and she never hurries this stage. The texture of the surface of the finished pot is important and she likes the burr thrown up by the grog when she scores lines. This gives depth and sharpness to the geometry of the decoration. To keep the surface features fresh, Jones uses no glaze but stains the clay with thin layers of metal oxides before firing to 2300°F (1260°C) in an electric kiln. This process gives the pots a dark, matt finish, with an occasional hint of luster, and the colors range from reddish-bronze through deep purples to solid black.

She finds that moving the pots around the studio and getting them into the kiln can be a problem. However, by keeping pots at a constant level when working, she is able to maneuver quite large ones without needing the strength to lift them. Details of her methods are described in 'Practical Considerations' on page 143.

Most of Jones' pots are between 18 and 36 in. (45 and 90 cm) in dimension, a size that she can handle by herself which fits comfortably into her kiln. Recently, she has had a number of commissions for larger work and this has necessitated a different approach.

A Commission for Large Pots

Jones was asked to make four very large pots for the Queen Elizabeth Conference Centre in London. These were to be between 58.5 and 70 in. (1.5 and 1.8 m) tall. It was not possible to make work of this scale in her studio or to fire it in her kiln, so she arranged to make the pots at a ceramics factory in Stoke-on-Trent. There they had kilns and forklift trucks for moving large-scale ceramics. Moving these enormous pots and installing them on site was done by a specialist contractor.

MICK ARNUP (UK)

Mick Arnup trained as a painter at Kingston College and at the Royal College of Art. He was already interested in ceramics during his time as a student, when he came under the influence of English studio potters such as Bernard Leach. In 1972, after a period of teaching, Arnup set up the workshop and showroom which he shares with his wife, the sculptor Sally Arnup.

He makes a range of stoneware pots including ornamental jars and large bowls on pedestals which often serve as planters. Like Jenifer Jones, he has been to Crete and seen traditional Cretan methods of making large pots. He feels that his jar forms are related to early Mediterranean and earthenware shapes. The jars are classical in form and are often decorated with sprigged sculptures. Sometimes he collaborates with his wife who makes sculptural attachments for his pots. The colors are a muted range of subtle red-browns or deep blue-greens which allow the sculptural details to speak for themselves.

Techniques

Arnup's large pots are made by assembling press-molded or thrown sections which are then finished by turning on a slow wheel. Arnup uses

Large thrown urn by Mick Arnup. With sprigged decoration, brushed with iron oxides and fired to 2336°F (1280°C).

coarse, robust clays such as Craft Crank, T-Material or his own recipe which includes Leeds Fireclay. He finishes the pots with either iron oxide or a matt blue-green ash glaze and fires them to 2336°F (1280°C) in reduction in a 70 cu. ft. (2 m³) oil-fired kiln.

Group of stoneware jars by Mick Arnup. Goat head attachments by Sally Arnup. On display at The Garden Gallery, Hampshire.

MONICA YOUNG (UK)

Monica Young is probably one of the best known makers of large pots in the UK. She was born in Paris and studied Fine Art in London and in Spain. She made a living by painting portraits and illustrating books, but always felt that working three-dimensionally would be exciting. She has been a potter since the 1970s, when she discovered coil pots. While teaching in a London school, she was required to teach a pottery lesson for an absent colleague and seeing the children coil pots intrigued her so much that she decided to try the method for herself and her life changed direction.

She set up her first studio in an outbuilding in Sussex and soon found that the focus of pottery in the 1970s was on throwing. There were no books or other sources of advice on coiling large pots. Through trial and error she pioneered her own methods and, within 18 months, she was exhibiting her work and selling through the Craft Potters Association. Young became an expert on making big coil pots and she now specializes in making enormous stoneware garden pots which can be up to 70 in. (1.8 m) in height.

In 1976 she moved to North Yorkshire and established her present workshop where she designed and built her own kiln, made all her own tools and devised the special equipment she needed for building her pots.

Diagram showing one of Monica Young's pots resting on wooden bars on a trolley. Selected bars can be removed to facilitate drying the base of the pot.

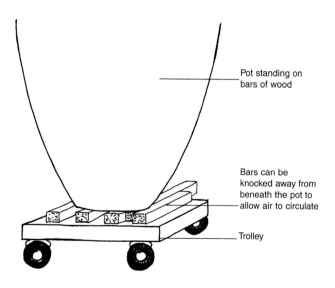

Pot standing on bars of wood

Bars can be knocked away from beneath the pot to allow air to circulate

Trolley

Techniques

Young's equipment includes a custom-built turntable, a large vertical pugmill, some stout step ladders, several trolleys and a winch-operated forklift (made by her local garage) which she uses to lift pots on the kiln trolley. She has made her own tools for working both inside and outside tall pots.

Each of her pots is built by coiling, using Potclays Craft Crank, and she starts their construction on a turntable. When a pot is finished it is transferred to a low, sturdy trolley to dry out. The trolleys are constructed from kitchen work-top board with heavy-duty castors fixed to the underside. Slats of wood of equal thickness are placed on the trolley to form a board for the base of the pot and selected slats are periodically knocked away and slid out from under the base to allow air to circulate underneath and facilitate drying. The pot ends up being supported on just two or three of these bars. When the pot is dry enough, it is wheeled to the kiln room. One of her pots can weigh as much as 378 lb. (175 kg).

Young works in two stages. First she builds the pot with stout coils to withstand the weight of the clay and to hold the shape. Because of the height of the pot, the base is coiled more thickly than the upper part. As the pot increases in height, she uses crepe bandages wound round the outside to support the coils and prevent the pot from collapsing outwards.

When coiling such tall pots it is essential to check that the pot is not leaning and Young does this by means of a plumb line suspended from a small gantry mounted on wheels. She starts checking when the pot is about 35 in. (90 cm) tall and beats the pot back into a true position using special paddling tools. This can sometimes slightly increase the diameter of the rim so a few more coils are added to curve the pot inwards again.

When she makes one of her tall overlapped pots she waits until it is about 49 in. (1.25 m) high before marking a vertical line where the overlap is to be positioned. She then slices right through the

OPPOSITE: Tall pots by Monica Young exhibited at The Hannah Peschar Sculpture Garden.
Photo: Hannah Peschar.

Monica Young making coils.

MonicaYoung adding coils to a tall pot which is supported with crêpe bandages.

A plumb line on a gantry is used to check that a tall pot is not listing.

wall of the pot along the mark to within 10 in. (25 cm) of the base and then gently pushes the left side inwards and pulls the right edge outwards ready for adding coils to make the overlap. After the overlap has been formed, the cut is repaired by adding coils to the inside to weld the seam together. Cutting is left to this late stage because tall narrow pots need frequent beating to keep them true and any protruding features would be destroyed by this process. The pot does not fall apart when sliced and pushed about because the clay has dried sufficiently for the walls to hold their shape. The surface of the pot is smoothed and more coils added to complete the full height.

When the pots are leatherhard, Young refines the shape by scraping away much of the excess clay, leaving the walls about 1 in. (2.5 cm) thick. She feels when she is refining and scraping the shape she is a sculptor, whereas when she is coiling the pot she is working as a potter.

Young has designed and made an ingenious set of tools. There are paddles made with sheep-

TOP LEFT: Group of paddles, some covered with sheepskin padding.
TOP RIGHT: Scrapers consisting of metal shim attached to wooden handles.
BOTTOM LEFT: Metal kidneys and other flat metal scrapers.
BOTTOM RIGHT: Needles mounted in wooden handles used for gauging the thickness of pot walls.

skin for beating the outside of a pot and anvils and curved pieces of wood for smoothing the inside. She uses a variety of long-handled tools to reach down and scrape the inside of a pot. Scraping tools include hoops of hacksaw blades, metal shim attached to wooden handles and long flexible saw blades which she uses bent into a curve to scrape downwards over large areas of the outside surface. To check that she is not scraping away too much clay and weakening the walls, she uses strong darning needles mounted in wooden handles to gauge thickness. She notes how much of the needle sticks out after being pushed through a wall. The needles are of varying lengths and she uses them to ensure that the base of the pot remains thicker and sturdier than the top section.

As the pot nears its full height Young works on a step ladder to reach the inside with her tools. An essential item is a long handled pincher similar to the one park-keepers use to pick up litter and she uses it to retrieve any dropped tools from the bottom of the pot. She also has scoops on long handles for collecting the scrapings from the inner walls which have fallen to the bottom of the pot.

Young pays a great deal of attention to the finishing of the rims and ridges on her pots. While the main surface has a slightly roughened texture,

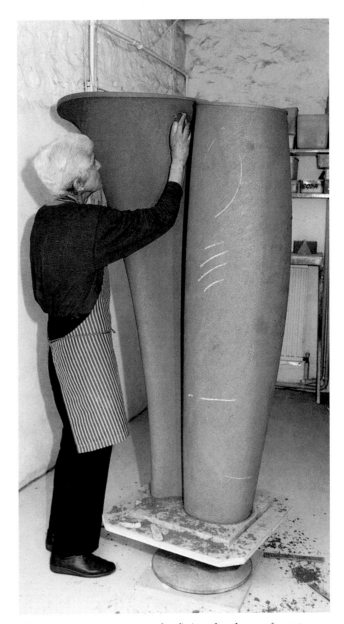

Monica Young scraping and refining the shape of a pot.

the rims and ridges are very smooth and polished. She compresses and polishes them with tools made from plastic credit cards or small pieces of plastic carton and finishes off with chamois leather.

It takes several weeks to build and dry a single pot before it can be fired. When the pot is ready for firing it is wheeled into the kiln room and transferred to her forklift platform. The platform and pot are then raised with a winding winch mechanism to the level of the kiln floor and the pot is eased into the kiln. The 100 cu. ft. (6 m³) trolley kiln is fired with eight burners using propane gas.

Young does not glaze her pots as she has found that the temperature difference between the top and bottom of her kiln is too large to give an even color to glazes. Instead she rubs chalk on the surface so that the pots acquire a toasted color when fired to 2381°F (1305°C) in a reducing atmosphere. She first used chalk to emphasize the pattern on some pots with incised decorative lines and was pleasantly surprised by the results. Now she uses chalk all the time.

Winch operated forklift which Monica Young uses for lifting pots to the kiln shelf.

LINDA JOHN (UK)

Linda John makes slip-decorated stoneware jars for gardens. These are not as large as Monica Young's pots, but she too views her pots as sculpture. Where Young has chosen a subtly textured, monochrome surface to emphasize her forms, John decorates her pots with colored imagery. She originally trained as a textile designer and she creates sophisticated patterns which flow around her pots.

She was inspired to make large urns after seeing two Nigerian women potters (Asibi Iddo and Asabe Magaji) demonstrate at one of the International Potters' Camps in Aberystwyth.

The symbolism of pots is important to John and she regards the round swelling urn shape as a metaphor for women and fecundity. She pays a great deal of attention to the external surface of her pots as she believes that the interior and exterior of a pot have different meanings.

Techniques

All John's work is handbuilt, usually by coiling. The clay body contains a high percentage of T-Material so that it will resist winter weather. The large urns are painted with colored slips and a thin wash of glaze is applied after bisque firing. The urns are fired one at a time in a top-loading electric kiln and John increases the height of the kiln with an extra layer of bricks under the lid to accommodate the taller pots. The tight fit and the weight of the urns makes packing the kiln awkward, as there is no room for her hands, so she uses a cloth sling to lower the urn into the kiln.

John has partly solved the problem of glazing such big pots through developing her own particular methods. The urns all have a hole in the bottom to allow drainage and prevent frost damage from accumulated water. This makes glazing the interior tricky. John's solution is to lay the urn on its side on the studio floor and pour glaze into it. She then rolls the urn backwards and

OPPOSITE: Coiled and slip decorated round urn by Linda John. H. 29 in. (75 cm).

forwards over the floor, taking care not to spill any glaze out of the hole in the bottom, while gradually altering the tilt of the pot to coat the whole of the inside. Emptying out the residual glaze is very difficult and John is considering attaching her urns to a concrete mixer in place of the cement mixing drum, but she has not yet tried out this idea.

The outside surfaces of the pots are painted with slips and left unglazed. After the final firing, the urns are painted with a transparent PVA sealant.

Although each of the potters in this chapter makes very different work, all of them view the pot form as something inherently beautiful which has its own place in a garden or landscape. A pot must be well-proportioned and big enough to have a significant presence in its surroundings, but there is no need for it to have any function other than to adorn the landscape.

'Flame' vase by Christine-Ann Richards (see Chapter 6). 23 x 19 in. (60 x 48 cm).

CHAPTER 5

BIRDBATHS, SUNDIALS AND LANTERNS

While some potters make pots which serve solely as ornament, others make garden ornaments which have a purpose, such as garden lanterns, bird feeders or sundial pedestals. This type of ornament became popular in Britain in the 19th century when the rapid increase in urbanization produced thousands of houses with gardens too small to accommodate grand fountains and statues, but with room for smaller items like birdbaths.

Sundials were probably the most prevalent of garden ornaments at this time. They have a very long history, stretching back into antiquity when they were the only means of telling the time and, even as recently as the 18th century, they were used to check the accuracy of clocks.

Bird-tables and birdbaths have become increasingly popular and may have originated with the feeding of pigeons, which were reared in lofts and dove-cotes to provide food for people. Birdbaths and feeders have become popular for small urban gardens as more people are taking an interest in birds and wildlife. It is possible that birdbaths derive from small fountains, since some early 20th century birdbaths are based on classical designs, often being a shell-like shallow basin on a fluted pedestal.

Other kinds of garden ornaments have developed alongside new ideas for gardens which have been introduced over the past 100 years. Gardening programs on television have promoted new design ideas, particularly for small town gardens. Japanese and Chinese gardens have influenced current garden styles and this can be seen in the work of potters such as Kate Mellors who is well known for her oriental garden lanterns.

Several British women potters, such as Kate Mellors, Christine-Ann Richards, Sarah Walton and myself, moved away from making small-scale thrown pots and adopted handbuilding techniques in the 1980s. We made this move quite independently of one another and, while it was partly prompted by our interest in gardens, I believe it was also a reaction against the prevailing orthodoxy of throwing and the restraints we felt this imposed on our work.

Sundial which belonged to the author's grandparents, Mr & Mrs E. J. Hessenberg.

KATE MELLORS (UK)

Kate Mellors trained as a studio potter in the 1970s, when to be a potter meant being a thrower. She was a succesful maker of thrown tableware until, after some 15 years, she became bored with the repetitive nature of the work. She began to develop ideas for garden pots after her parents asked her to make them some plant pots and an outdoor lantern. They had a garden which contained different varieties of bamboo and interesting structures, and her architect father admired Japanese buildings. This gave her ideas for garden lanterns and since these sold well she soon gave up tableware to make garden pots.

Her range of work now includes birdbaths, self-circulating fountains, planters and urns, tables, stools, sundial bases and stepping stones, as well as lanterns.

Garden lanterns in blue matt glaze by Kate Mellors.

Techniques

Mellors makes her garden pots using a combination of methods including throwing, slabbing and press molding. She has a powerful Fitzwilliam electric wheel, a Roderveld slab roller and a vertical pugmill which all contribute to efficient production. She also has a dehumidifier to help dry her pots in winter.

She uses two clays from Potclays, mixed together in different proportions according to what is being made. For slab-built pots she uses equal parts of Craft Crank clay and Camberwell Buff clay, while for throwing she mixes two parts of Craft Crank with three parts Camberwell Buff. She throws with very soft clay, often mixing the reclaimed slops with fresh clay and she makes large pots over a period of two or three days. A thick, freshly-thrown section is added to a stiffened, previously thrown base and then she continues throwing to the final size. The throwing is carefully finished and smoothed so that she only has a little turning to do later.

The lanterns are made using slabs, molds and throwing. The roofs are constructed by cutting six slabs which are rolled so that they are thinner towards the top of the roof. The slabs are then put into a press mold and joined with thick coils. The roof comes out of the mold fairly rough and the shape is smoothed and refined. A finial is thrown directly on to the roof of the small lanterns, while large lanterns have a finial which is thrown separately and joined to the roof later. The roof is placed upside down on a large flower pot with padding round the edge so that the thrown body of the lantern can be attached and the windows cut out. The lanterns sit on pedestals of various styles which are either made from thrown sections or slab-built.

The pots are left for a week or two to dry naturally in the workshop before being moved into the kiln room to dry out completely. When fully dry they are raw glazed with a matt glaze containing a high percentage of clay. The glaze is applied in two coats with a sponge. For her blue glaze, Mellors adds cobalt and iron to the base recipe and for the sandstone glaze she adds yellow iron oxide. The work is fired very slowly in a propane gas kiln of about 35 cu. ft. (1 m³) capacity. The firing takes ten to 12 hours to reach 752°F (400°C) and then a further 13 hours to reach 2336°F (1280°C). She gives the kiln a light reduction for about two hours at the end. There is a wide range of color with the blue glaze from a rather bright blue to a more subdued green-brown hue which is probably due to variations in the atmosphere of each firing. The firing temperature makes her work frostproof but, as Craft Crank has quite an open body, she adds the buff clay as an extra precaution against any chance of water penetration. She advises her customers to empty fountains in the winter.

While the influence of Japan is clearly visible in the design of her lanterns, Mellors gets inspiration from many other sources, such as Nigerian wood carving, architectural metalwork from English churches and large Cretan pots. She does not envision making a return to thrown tableware as her move to making garden ornaments and planters has been very successful.

Kate Mellors working on the roof section of a lantern.

SARAH WALTON (UK)

Sarah Walton originally studied painting and her main interest was in landscape. However, she developed a strong desire to work in three-dimensions and so enrolled in the influential Studio Pottery course at Harrow School of Art. Her thrown, salt-glazed domestic pots were soon highly regarded and much sought after. In the 1980s Walton started working on a larger scale because of her interest in form and natural light. In 1990 she won the Guild of St George John Ruskin Award which enabled her to develop large handbuilt forms for open-air settings.

Walton makes birdbaths for gardens as she feels that these are a form of sculpture that convey her intent through form and light. They combine her interest in landscape with the effects of firing which transforms the soft, mud-like clay into a hard stone. Light interacts with the solid form through reflection in the water held in the birdbath.

The birdbaths are salt fired and come in four different colors and effects. They are then mounted on wood block bases which are of several types of wood and range in height from 8 in. (20 cm) to 30 in. (75 cm).

Salt-glazed birdbaths mounted on wood blocks by Sarah Walton. Exhibited at the Harley Gallery, Nottinghamshire. *Photo: Courtesy of the Harley Gallery.*

Sarah Walton pressing clay into a mold to make a section of a birdbath.

Techniques

Walton press-molds the birdbaths in plaster molds using her own clay body mixture, for which the recipe is:

- 25 Grolleg china clay
- 50 fireclay
- 25 Hyplas 71 ball clay
- 5 Quartz (200s mesh)
- 35 sand, grog, molochite (10 finer than 80s mesh, 25 over 80s mesh)

She starts by pressing very soft clay into two-piece molds. When the clay is leatherhard the sections are lifted out of the molds and refined by hand, both before and after assembling the pieces. Moving the completed birdbaths is done with the help of a foldable winch-operated platform. An assistant helps with packing and unloading the kiln.

All the birdbaths are first decorated with slips which are simple combinations of ball clay, china clay and red clay, and then salt fired to temperatures between 2264°–2372°F (1240°–1300°C).

There is no biscuit firing so the raw pots need a long preheating stage using gas. This is followed by an oil-fueled firing with a reducing atmosphere between 1796°F (980°C) and 2264°F (1240°C). Salt is put into the kiln between 2048°F (1120°C) and 2336°F (1280°C).

The salt-glazed clay body is vitrified stoneware which ensures that the birdbaths are frostproof. The design of the birdbaths is such that only a shallow pool of water ever forms in them and this pool has room to expand on freezing, thus preventing cracking.

Detail of a birdbath, by Sarah Walton, showing a shallow depression which fills with rain water.
Photo: Robin Parrish.

KARIN HESSENBERG (UK)

After 15 years as a thrower, I had become frustrated with working on the wheel, feeling that it constricted my ideas, and I wanted to make larger forms. While my pots are ornamental, I feel that it is important that they are used and are part of everyday life.

I added birdbaths and sundials to my range of garden planters because they are fairly large and provide an opportunity to make interesting forms. The birdbath is made from two parts, a three-tier pedestal and a separate top which fits into the pedestal after both sections have been fired. The birdbaths are usually tall to prevent cats reaching the birds, but I occasionally make smaller ones in response to customer requests. I advise

Birdbath with green slip glaze by Karin Hessenberg. H. 28 in. (72 cm).

customers to place their birdbaths in an open position away from places where cats can hide and pounce on the birds.

My sundials have simpler decoration than my planters because part of the decoration is in the brass plate. Instead of a patterned texture, the sundials have simple sprigs which are stylized leaf or flower motifs based on Victorian cast iron work.

Techniques

I use Potclays Craft Crank clay to make garden pots. These are all handbuilt from slabs cut from blocks of clay using a wire stretched between notched sticks. The main advantage of this method is that space for a large slab roller is not required. Rolling, on the other hand, compresses the clay and this gives it extra strength when fired.

I pick up the cut slabs on a rolling pin and lay them on sheets of newspaper spread on wooden boards. I then put templates made of stiff cardboard or thin plywood on to the slabs and draw around them with a pointed knife to mark out the necessary pieces. Sometimes I press patterns into the marked areas, using plaster blocks or stamps of my own design.

I raw glaze my work when it is completely dry and I wax the bottoms of the pots because it is difficult to clean glaze off unfired clay. The wax is a semi-liquid floor cleaning polish and I pour a small

Sundial, reactive slips and white glaze by Karin Hessenberg. H. 28 in. (72 cm).

Blue patio lantern by Karin Hessenberg. H. 14 in. (36 cm).

Working sequence *All photos: Robin Parrish.*

Stage 1: Beating a block of clay into the correct size and shape.

Stage 2: Checking the size of the clay block with a cardboard template.

Stage 3: Cutting the slabs with a wire stretched between notched cutting sticks.

Stage 4: Lifting a slab on a rolling pin.

Stage 5: Laying the slab on a sheet of newspaper to dry out.

Stage 6: Shape of pot section drawn on slab using a template and pointed knife.

A patterned plaster block is pressed into the soft slab to make the texture on the pot.

Small wood blocks with nail points which are pulled along a ruler guide to comb lines either 1 in. or 0.5 in. (2.5 cm or 1.25 cm) apart.

Combing the strips along a ruler. The 1 in. (2.5 cm). strips of clay are used to make the joins between the tiers of tall pots and the 0.5 in. (1.25 cm) strips make the beading on the outside of the pieces.

amount into a pottery jar which I stand in very hot water. This warms the wax and makes it more fluid for ease of application. I then apply the glazes with a sponge. I fire my work slowly to Orton cone 9 (2300°F/1260°C) in an electric kiln. I have a Safefire 5000 programmer and the cycle is set at 95°F (35°C) per hour to 392°F (200°C) with the kiln vent open. This is followed by 185°F (85°C) per hour to 1112°F (600°C) and then 302°F (150°C) per hour to 2300°F (1260°C) set end point followed by a half hour soak period. I close the vent at about 1472°F (500°C).

STEFFANIE SAMUELS (USA)

Totemic sculptures, human busts and figures, life murals, decorated relief wall planters and ceramic birdbaths are all part of Steffanie Samuels' wide range of work. Her inspiration comes from a variety of sources including cartoons, mythical legends and Eastern religions. Her ceramics are intended to be fanciful and fun as well as functional. She loves gardening and sees her birdbaths as ornaments in a garden setting.

Techniques

The birdbaths are made from a strong stoneware clay body suitable for sculpture. The pedestals are made from three thrown sections which are joined together when leatherhard while the basin of the birdbath is slab built in a press mold. The rim is formed by adding a coil to the slab and smoothed by throwing. A foot is thrown on to the underside of the basin which makes it fit snugly into

'Bird Cat' Bath by Steffanie Samuels. H. 33 in. (84 cm).

the top of the pedestal. Some of the sculptural decoration is coiled and modeled on to the surface of the form before it is fired while other parts, such as the sculptures that sit in the birdbath, are made separately by coiling, slabbing and modeling. These are attached to the birdbath after firing with epoxy resin and silicone caulk.

The birdbath basins and pedestals are bisque fired before being sprayed with black porcelain slip which is built up in layers until the surface appears granular. The birdbaths are brushed with glossy and cratered glazes and fired to cone 8 (2282°F/1250°C) in an electric kiln. The basins are fired in saggars to prevent warping.

To install the birdbaths, a rod is hammered securely into the ground and the pedestal is lowered over it; this prevents the birdbath from tipping. The foot of the basin is fitted into the top of the pedestal. Making the birdbath in two sections makes transport easier and also enables easy cleaning. Samuels advises that the birdbath basin is protected against frost in winter either by draining it and storing it upside down in plastic, or by bringing it indoors. The pedestal can be left outside.

Steffanie Samuels working on a birdbath basin.

HOLLY HANESSIAN (USA)

Birdbaths and birdhouses comprised a series of sculptural pieces for garden settings that Holly Hanessian made between 1993 and 1996. Although she regards her work as sculpture, she also likes it to have a function. She is a keen gardener so it seemed natural to combine her sculpture with gardening. She aims to make work that is visually exciting and that will work within the elements of a garden setting. She has traveled widely and has been inspired by wood-carved sculptures from regions as far apart as West Africa and the Pacific Rim islands.

Holly Hanessian assembling a birdhouse.

Stage 1: Fitting the base section on to the metal support rod using nuts and washers.

Techniques

Hanessian is very involved with textured surfaces in clay and uses a variety of techniques to achieve the effects she wants. She often uses a wire tool to cut facets in the bases of her forms, while effects similar to hand-forged ironwork are obtained by twisting pieces of clay over a wooden dowel. She uses clay of differing consistencies, sometimes applying very soft, sticky clay to the surface of a form and then adding a very thick vitreous slip. The work is colored with thin washes of stain and underglaze after the biscuit firing, and a thin transparent glaze is applied. This develops the colors and protects the surface. Blues and greens are produced using another glaze.

Hanessian's birdbaths and houses are usually 46 to 58.5 in. (1.2 to 1.5 m) tall and consist of ceramic shapes stacked on a threaded metal rod. She developed this technique of assembling smaller shapes on a rod to form large objects because her kiln is rather small, and this method also meant that she can easily lift the modules into position.

She has two main methods for stacking her ceramic sculptures. The first is to assemble pieces on a threaded metal rod which runs through all the sections as described for the birdbath. The rod is held in place by means of a nut and washer in the top and bottom sections while rubber washers are used to cushion the joints. The middle sections are stacked over

Stage 2: Sliding a pedestal section on to the support rod.

Stage 3: Securing another pedestal section on the support rod by tightening a nut.

Stage 4: Fitting the final piece of the birdhouse to the support.

71

Birdhouse by Holly Hanessian.

Hanessian's transparent glaze has a wide firing temperature range. All the work is fired to cone 6, approximately 2192°F (1200°C). The sculptures are constructed from either of two clay bodies. One is based on Carbondale Red Clay with fireclay and additions of grog, while the other body (provided by the potter Val Cushing) is for use in cold climates. Some of her favorite glaze recipes have also been given by fellow potters.

Carbondale clay recipe (cone 6)

Custer Feldspar	8
AP Green Fireclay	30
CC ball clay	12
Carbondale Red clay	40
Grog	10

Vitreous slip (cone 6)

Custer Feldspar	10
Nepheline syenite	10
Ball clay	30
Edgar plastic kaolin	20
Flint	30

Ron Meyer's transparent glaze (cone 04-4 but used at cone 6)

Frit 3124 (ferro)	72.73
Bentonite	9.09
Edgar plastic kaolin	9.09
Flint	9.09

Andy Martin's glaze (cone 6)

Nepheline syenite	30
Barium carbonate	32
Strontium carbonate	18
Frit 3110 (ferro)	6
6 tile clay	3
Bentonite	4
Flint	4

Oxides are added to the Andy Martin glaze recipe to obtain different shades of green or blue. For chartreuse green add 0.5% chrome oxide; for turquoise add 4% copper carbonate; for dark blue add 3% copper carbonate plus 0.25% cobalt carbonate.

the rod with rubber washers between them to act as buffers. The base section is heavy while the middle and top sections are lighter so that the sculpture is stable. The sections are prevented from slipping around on the rod by making an internal clay tube through each one. This tube is made on a dowel rod slightly larger than the metal threaded rod. The clay sections are built on the dowel rod and, when the clay is leatherhard, the wooden dowel is removed and the metal rod substituted. To ensure that the sculpture does not lean from the vertical, a magnetic level is attached to the top of the metal rod and regular checks are made. After the bisque firing the stack is checked for a secure fit and any adjustments can be made by sanding or filing the sections.

The second method uses gravity and interlocking sections to build the sculpture. The sections fit into each other by means of a conical male end on the upper side of the base section slotting into a matching female hollow in the bottom of the next section of the sculpture. For an accurate fit, these male and female shapes are made in plaster molds. As the sculpture is built up it is checked to ensure that it is level and, as with the first method, the base is heavier and thicker than the top. For installation outdoors the pieces are fixed with epoxy resin adhesive.

Su Lupasco (UK)

Su Lupasco uses metal and many other materials in the construction of her garden ceramics which include birdbaths, sundials, archways and wall reliefs. These other materials, which include wood and concrete, are not just hidden supports for clay modules, but are a visible and integral part of the form. Lupasco uses throwing, slabbing, press-molding, coiling and modeling techniques and, in addition, welds metal or fixes parts with adhesives.

Birdbath by Su Lupasco. H. 39 in. (1 m).

Lupasco has a vivid imagination and she often experiments with found objects and materials. Her sundial with a piece of farm machinery for the pedestal is a good example of this.

Techniques

Lupasco uses a clay body which is a mix of either T-Material with St Thomas or T-Material with white stoneware. She colors her work by brushing on engobes or slips in shades of red and turquoise which she selectively sponges off to give variations in color and texture. She has favorite glazes such as lithium and barium blues

Sundial incorporating old farm equipment by Su Lupasco. H. 51 in. (1.3 m).

and Potterycrafts Gold Glaze, and likes to make the colors look layered, worn and old. Lupasco has two electric kilns, a small one of 0.05 m³ (2 cu. ft.) and a large one which is 0.3 m³ (12 cu. ft.) She bisques and glaze fires pieces at the same time because the firing temperature is relatively low at around 1976°F (1080°C).

Because of the porous nature of the clay body and the rough, textured character of her work, Lupasco applies many coats of builders' waterproofing fluid to her pieces to ensure that they are frostproof.

In the 1970s some potters regarded joining ceramic pieces with adhesives, rather than by firing, as 'cheating'. These inhibitions have been abandoned and makers are now using strong adhesives, such as epoxy resins, to build sundials or bird feeders from sections stacked over metal posts. We have seen this technique demonstrated by Holly Hanessian on page 71. Robin

Sundial by Robin Welch.

Welch's sundial and bird feeder, illustrated below, are also good examples of this type of construction.

This ability to stack ceramic modules over a rod or pipe, coupled with a supply of flexible plastic tubing and small electric pumps, has also led many potters to design fountains and water features which will be the subject of the next chapter.

Bird feeder by Robin Welch.

CHAPTER 6

FOUNTAINS
AND WATER FEATURES

P onds, water gardens and small fountains are now so popular in small gardens that it is easy to forget that these features would not have been possible without the introduction of a piped domestic water supply and the invention of hoses and small electric pumps. In the past water for gardens was stored in rain barrels and tanks or collected from wells and streams. Large estates or gardens had their own streams or irrigation canals which had to be controlled regularly and so, until the 19th century, ornamental gardens were the prerogative of the wealthy. Even so, gardens were functional as well as for pleasure, with kitchen gardens and fish ponds providing food.

Ponds and lakes were ornamental features in grand landscaped gardens and, before mechanical pumps were invented, fountains depended on water being raised by hydraulics and gravity, usually from a water source located high above the lake. Few gardens had sufficient water pressure to operate fountains successfully. Such large projects depended on skilled water engineers and could usually only be undertaken by the nobility. Vast schemes like that at Versailles involved huge expense, but the hydraulic

Fountain in Bassin d'Apollon, Versailles, France.
Photo: Robin Parrish.

problems were never satisfactorily resolved and the fountains could not all perform at their best simultaneously. For this reason, servants were obliged to rush around the grounds when Louis XIV took a walk, switching on fountains as he approached while other servants followed behind, turning off the ones he had already seen.

Fountains have a long history. They have been recorded in the gardens of ancient Assyria; there are fountains in paintings of Roman gardens at Pompeii; and they are depicted in Roman mosaics. Water is also central to Islamic gardens and among the best examples are the Generalife gardens of the Alhambra Palace in Spain. Fountains are imbued with symbolism because clean water was prized in times when people died from drinking contaminated water. Pure water from springs and wells meant health and life and came to represent purity. In both the Islamic and Christian worlds, fountains have three symbolic elements. They represent the source of life, cleansing and wisdom. This is reflected in the design of the fountain with its three states of water: the bubbling source welling up; the flowing, cleansing stream; and the still, silent pool of wisdom.

Largely because of these symbolic elements, many fountains are made to designs which date back thousands of years. Many medieval European fountains have lion or leopard heads

Fountain in Patio de los Leones, Alhambra, Spain. *Photo: Robin Parrish.*

which may have been introduced by crusaders returning from Islamic lands. Lion heads persist as a stylistic motif today, not only on fountains but on garden planters and other ornaments.

Sculpture forms an integral part of the great fountains of European palaces built during the 17th and 18th centuries. There are few modern gardens which have anything on this scale and the largest fountains are likely to be found in public squares, gardens or parks.

However small fountains for domestic gardens have become very popular and this has provided opportunities for artists and designers. Fountains now come in a great variety of styles, from simple sprays in the center of a pond to abstract sculptures with water as part of the overall form.

Some designers have borrowed ideas from Japan. There, water features are often visually discreet and artfully natural in contrast to the European fountains which are designed to be focal points. In Japan, controlling moving water is an art form and there are even specialists who adjust the water flow to obtain pleasing musical notes.

In the last 20 years potters have become increasingly involved with this trend and are making exciting and innovative fountains and water features.

KATE MALONE (UK)

Symbolism is important to Kate Malone and fountains, with their inherent meanings, provide an ideal way of expressing her ideas. Her work is inspired by living forms and colors and almost every aspect of her work contains symbolic meaning. She has made many pieces based on sea creatures and fish and her many colored glazes reflect the blues and greens of water. She fires the glazes so that they acquire fluidity, with colors running and melting together and even forming drips off rims and projections.

Her giant sculptures of multi-colored fish are now a familiar part of the landscape at Hackney Marshes in London. The fish are in the middle of a lake and their heads and tails rise out of the water as if the fish are coming up for air. Although they are not fountains they are a feature made for a water setting. Malone's fish fountains establish an even clearer link between aquatic creatures and water.

It is not so easy to see how fruit-shaped jugs relate to the symbolism of moving water but it is no accident that many of Malone's fountains are jug forms. Jugs are traditionally containers for nourishing, life-giving drinks while fruit represents immortality, containing as it does the seed of the next generation. This links the jugs with the meaning of fountains as a source of life.

Malone used these aspects of jugs and fruit when making a commission for Homerton Hospital in

Courtyard fountain by Kate Malone at The Royal Devon and Exeter Hospital. Two fish, multi-colored earthenware glazes.

London. This is a water feature called 'Life Pours Forth' and is a large jug pouring water into a bowl – it is intended to be an image of rejuvenation and water as the source of life.

Notes on Fountains

Fountains are more complicated than large planters or sculptural works because the electricity and water supplies have to be considered. Several other factors also need to be taken into account including:

• Evaporation: With small fountains that use the same water recycled through the system, it is important to specify or carry out regular maintenance checks as evaporation can be surprisingly high. This relates to the number of jets and their size, but a bucket of water may be needed on a hot day to replenish even a small fountain. Where possible there should be an automatic refill system.

• Electricity: Safety precautions are vital for an outdoor electrical supply and advice should always be sought from a qualified electrician. Cable extensions and other accessories can be obtained from pump suppliers.

• Water Jets: The aesthetics of the water jets need to be considered – whether there is to be a

'Rise and Shine Magic Fish' by Kate Malone. Sculptures in Hackney Marshes, Lea Valley Nature Reserve, London. Crystalline glazes on T-Material fired to 2300°F (1260°C).

lively sprinkle or a smooth flow of water. Nozzles for the jets can be custom-made or bought ready-made in a variety of styles. The sound of the water is important as a noisy drip or splash can be irritating.

• Pumps: There is no single easy way of selecting a fountain pump. It must be powerful enough to do the job and also be silent. A noisy pump can ruin the feeling of peace and tranquility that one expects from a fountain.

Kate Malone mentions two methods of matching pumps to fountains. The first is to buy a pump and try it out in a bucket of water or in a pond. The fountain can then be designed with a full knowlege of the flow and height of the water that can be obtained with a particular pump. Good quality pumps can be bought from garden centers at a variety of prices, and generally the more expensive ones are more reliable. Pumps vary in performance so thorough trials are important.

The second method is to design and make the fountain and specify the volume of water to be moved per minute, and over what distance or head. Then locate a pump supplier and give them the precise

Detail of bronze drinking fountain by Kate Malone in Castle Park, Bristol. Pressing the eye of a fish on the side of the piece operates the water jets.

specifications. With large projects and big budgets it is best to call in the experts as it is a specialist job to engineer a large water project.

Techniques

Malone handbuilds her work using T-Material, a clay body which fires white to provide a bright base for the glazes. It is versatile at both earthenware and stoneware temperatures. She uses three basic forming techniques: press molding, coiling and hand modeling, and many of her pots are made in two stages.

The body part is usually press molded in a two-piece plaster mold which she has made from a coiled master shape. She fills the two halves of the mold with small slabs of clay which are all of the same thickness and joins them carefully to ensure an even thickness of clay in the mold. When both parts of the mold are filled they are left to dry until the clay is leatherhard. Malone takes care that the edges do not dry out too much by protecting them with strips of plastic wrap. When satisfied that the molded parts are sufficiently strong, she turns them out of the molds and joins them together. The base is then finished off and the surface tidied up, ready for the addition of coils to form the upper section.

Malone rolls the coils by hand as they have more strength than extruded ones and, to prevent them drying too much, she only rolls out one at a time. She cross-hatches between each coil but does not use water or slip for joining as she works with soft clay. Over a period of days the rims of the pots dry and strengthen enough to take further layers of coils. The coils are smoothed together with the thumb and bumps are scraped away with a piece of hacksaw blade. She finishes smoothing the surface with a thick rubber kidney.

Low-relief decoration is applied by adding sprigs or by modeling directly on to the pot. With hand-modeling, pieces of clay are roughly applied to the surface of the pot and then shaped through plastic wrap. She finds that making marks through various thicknesses of plastic gives a very interesting 'soft look' to the surface and even mundane tools create interesting effects.

All Malone's work is dried out very carefully and wrapped in plastic to allow the moisture content to equalize. It may be weeks before very large pieces are unwrapped, particularly if soft clay has been modeled on to a firm body. Once unwrapped, large pots require regular turning to avoid uneven drying caused by draughts.

Malone makes large items on kiln shelves: she has three extra large kiln shelves that were specially ordered. This makes moving the delicate pot easier as it can be lifted on the shelf, although this usually requires three or four people.

Malone previously worked with multi-fired earthenware glazes and, although she still uses them on certain pieces, she is now working with crystalline glazes fired to stoneware temperature. Both earthenware and stoneware glazes are used very thickly and applied with big, soft glaze brushes and mops.

The earthenware glazes are applied to a high fired bisque body (2156°F/1180°C) before firing several times to 1868°–1976°F (1020°–1080°C). She likes to use thick layers of glaze but these can be difficult to apply to a high-fired bisque body, so the glaze is mixed to a thick consistency and put through a 100s mesh sieve before it is thickened further with calcium chloride. She buys the calcium chloride in flake form, fills a jam jar with about 3 in. (7 cm) of the flakes and then adds an equal amount of boiling water to dissolve them. The calcium chloride works by turning the glaze mixture into a colloidal gel of the consistency of yogurt. The thickened glaze can be stored and in this state it can be picked up on a soft brush and smeared on to the pot.

The earthenware glazes are mixed from one or two commercially prepared base glazes with a wide firing range. Coloring oxides or pigments are added to the base glaze. Malone also uses some ready-mixed wet glazes for special effects and colors. A pot may be fired three or four times with new colors added at each stage. The bottom of the pot is glazed only for the last firings, with the pot set on large stilts. Sharp areas and drips are ground off with an angle grinder fitted with a diamond-edged disk.

The crystalline glazes are fired to stoneware (2300°–2336°F/1260°–1280°C) in a carefully controlled firing cycle involving very slow cooling between 1997°F and 1956°F (1093°C and 1069°C). Malone uses two or three recipes developed by Emmanuel Cooper and Derek Clarkson as the

bases for her different colored crystalline glazes. She paints the glazes in very thick layers on the bisque-fired pot using her soft brushes. The crystalline glazes are extremely runny at top temperature, so the pots are fired in specially made trays to catch the pools of glaze. The pots have to be chiselled out of the trays and the bases are then ground with various grinders and diamond pads. A scarred base is often finished with gold leaf.

Occasionally Malone has her work cast in bronze when it is to be installed in public places where vandalism could be a problem. She makes the piece in clay, biscuit fires it and then delivers it to the foundry. The foundry takes a mold from this master and casts it using the lost wax method. The biscuit original is then returned to Malone who refires it to remove any dirt and grease. It is then glazed and the client is presented with both the glazed clay piece and the bronze copy.

There is always a risk that the master will get damaged while the mold is being taken, but this risk is reduced by presenting the foundry with a biscuit-fired rather than a raw piece. It is important to check the wax cast from the mold of the original as the bronze can only be as good as the wax cast. The more bronzes cast from one original, the lower the single unit cost as the mold costs are dispersed. Patination of the surface can be done by the foundry or the artist. Weathering and usage also patinate the piece.

Fixing a finished fountain into position is carried out by professional contractors.

Kate Malone at work in her studio.

CHRISTINE-ANN RICHARDS (UK)

Christine-Ann Richards is inspired by both Chinese pottery and Japanese water features. She is well-known for her thrown porcelain but around 1990 she started making large handbuilt earthenware pots for plants and gardens. She felt the need to move away from throwing and to work on a much larger scale. Her interest in Far Eastern ceramics led to her gaining a Churchill Fellowship to travel to Japan to study water features. This experience has assisted her in developing a range of self-contained water gardens which are intended for patios, conservatories and small gardens.

Richards' water gardens are made from interlocking modules which allow her to build simple or more complex forms. The simplest water gardens consist of a tall pot with a loose fitting ceramic tray which sits inside to cover the pump and support aquatic plants. Some of these water gardens have a glass tray and a submerged halogen lamp so that light can shine up through the water and move with the ripples created by the pump. The more sophisticated water gardens have waterfalls which cascade into the main container. A matching planter can be placed on top so that foliage trails down the waterfall. Some water-

falls may have one or more small holes, while others have a thin slit which allows the water to seep silently down the side of the module, creating a permanent gleam on the surface of the clay.

Although Richards' water features owe much to Japanese ideas, the decoration on her pots is related to Chinese calligraphy. All her garden pots are made of a high-firing earthenware clay and some are in a single plain color while others have different colored clays marbled together to produce calligraphic marks. These are usually combinations of black clay with white clay, black with red, or red with white.

Like Malone, Richards has thoroughly tested pumps through trial and error, often by walking round garden centers to see how quiet the displayed pumps are.

As well as water gardens Richards also makes planters, tall ornamental vases and sculptural pieces for open-air locations. All this work is large and heavy and she had to adapt her working methods and kiln when she changed from making thrown porcelain. She has developed her own methods of building and firing large pots.

Techniques

The garden pots are coiled and press molded using combinations of different colored Dutch earthenware clays produced by Vingerling and available from Potterycrafts Ltd. Some of the pots are started in three-piece molds which were made by a professional mold maker. Each mold has a floor section and two sides. Slabs and coils of clay are pressed into the molds and smoothed together. When the pot is stiff enough to support itself, the sides of the mold are removed. The pot is lifted off the plaster base on to a kiln shelf which rests on a kiln base on castors. The clay comes out of the mold with a smooth surface which she roughens with a surform blade to bring out the grogged texture.

Pebbles piled up to hide leads and water outlet

Electric leads

Pump

Glass tray which supports pebbles

Halogen lamp

Diagram of a simple water garden with a halogen lamp and glass tray.

OPPOSITE: Black and red waterfall garden by Christine-Ann Richards. H. 43 in. (1.1 m), with a steep planter, H. 23 in. (60 cm).
Photo: Geoffrey Onyett.

Christine-Ann Richards building a tall pot on a kiln base.
All photos: Sally Pollitzer

ABOVE LEFT: Step 1: The first section of the top-hat kiln being lowered over the partly built pot. The top of the pot is covered with plastic wrap to keep it moist for joining further coils.

ABOVE RIGHT: Step 2: The sides of the kiln are protected with cloths while Richards roughs the surface of the clay with a surform to bring up the grog.

ABOVE LEFT: Step 3: Richards uses kneeling boards placed on the kiln as she builds more coils on to the pot. Bandages support the shape of the pot.

ABOVE RIGHT: Step 4: Richards beats the pot into a smooth shape using a butter pat as a paddle.

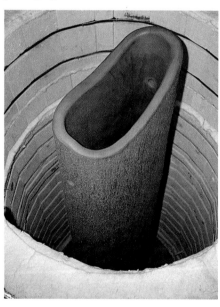

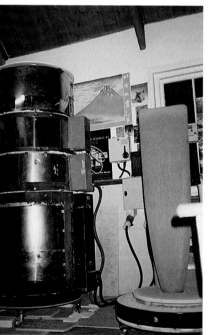

ABOVE LEFT: Step 5: The tall pot stands inside two sections of the top-hat kiln and the third kiln section is lifted into place by means of a hoist.

ABOVE RIGHT: Looking down at the pot in the kiln which now has three wall sections in position.

ABOVE LEFT: The complete top-hat kiln ready for firing. The three main sections each have independent electrical controllers. A tall pot on another kiln base stands next to the kiln.

ABOVE RIGHT: A fired tall pot being hoisted out of the kiln using a pulley and chain.

Richards builds her very tall pots directly on to a kiln shelf on a kiln base, so that she can use a top-hat kiln and avoid lifting very heavy work. Top-hat kilns are well-known in the USA but none of the leading kiln manufacturers in Britain produce them, so she decided to reconstruct her Potterycrafts electric top-loader as a top-hat kiln when she moved house and studio. She converted the kiln with the aid of staff from Bath Potters' Supplies, together with an electrician and a structural engineer.

The base was adapted with extra strong castors to take the weight of the large pots and the side section ring of the kiln was reinforced so that it could be lifted on a hand-operated chain hoist and lowered over the pot on the kiln base. Richards has increased the height of her kiln by adding extra side rings and she can now fire pots that are 58.5 in. (1.5 m) tall. These extra kiln sections each have their own power supply.

She made extra kiln bases from brick kiln lids and put them on castors so that she can work on two or three pots at one time. Tall pots such as her Wave Form sculptures are made directly on to a kiln base and then the first ring section of kiln is lowered over the partly built pot. Further coils are added before the next section of kiln is lowered. Working next to the kiln Richards completes the form before lowering the top section of kiln over it.

Since the pot is built inside the kiln, she is obliged to use the kiln as a drying cabinet before proceeding to the firing cycle. The kiln is controlled by a Cambridge 202 programmer; drying and firing takes about 60 hours. A typical cycle would be to fire the kiln overnight at 9°F (5°C) per hour then all the next day at 18°F (10°C) per hour with the lid off; overnight at 27°F (15°C) per hour with the lid on but slightly ajar; then with the lid closed and bung in and the temperature rising steadily throughout the second day to 1112°F (600°C) by evening. The kiln is finally fired to reach 2102°F (1150°C) by the third morning.

Richards' pots are made frostproof by the firing temperature and by sealing them with a silicone fluid sealant after they have been fired.

RIGHT: Ceramic terrazzo fountain by Felicity Aylieff.

FELICITY AYLIEFF (UK)

Although Aylieff is primarily a sculptor (see Chapter 9), she has designed a large fountain intended for a courtyard setting. Her fountain is constructed in the same way as her sculptures, by use of molds and with bright colored inclusions in the clay body to give a terrazzo effect on the surface. In this piece water flows evenly down the sides of the fountain, creating a sheen and enhancing the colors in the terrazzo, just as a wet stone has brighter colors than a dry one.

Detail of ceramic terrazzo showing colored inclusions by Felicity Aylieff.

CERAMIC TERRAZZO FOUNTAIN – SECTION VIEW

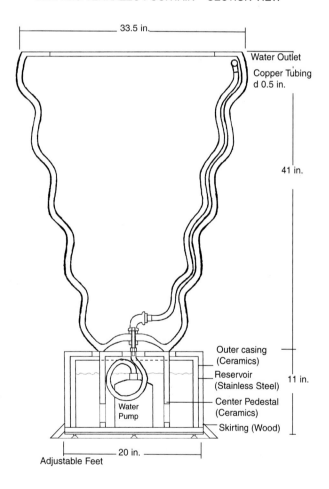

Diagram of fountain showing pump connections and water pipe. By Felicity Aylieff.

ROBIN WELCH (UK)

Welch is better known for his sculptural thrown stoneware vessels. Recently, however, inspired by his own garden, he has developed larger scale garden work.

His garden pieces, constructed from precisely thrown sections with concentric bands of color, are reminiscent of the precision of the functional jigger and jolleyed forms he produced in the 1970s. These garden pieces are sculptures built from interlocking modules which can function as a fountain, birdbath or sundial (see Chapter 5).

Tall fountain by Robin Welch comprising a series of ever diminishing inverted bowls supported on a pillar. Water rains down from beneath the top bowl and cascades over the lower ones to drip into the pebble covered pool. The work is made of high fired stoneware in a controlled palette of colors which emphasise the form.

DAVID AND MARGARET FRITH (UK)

David Frith is inspired by the landscape of North Wales where he and his wife, Margaret Frith, established their workshop 35 years ago. Frith's work is thrown in stoneware clay and reduction fired. He uses traditional techniques but regards himself as a contemporary potter who seeks a timeless quality in his work. His pieces are individual and often large, and include planters, bottles, ginger jars, store jars and pressed and extruded dishes. He likes flat surfaces which lend themselves to being decorated with layers of glazes and wax resist motifs.

His fountains developed as an extension of the pots and the making processes are similar. They are all handthrown, made from Frith's own stoneware body, and fired in a reduction gas kiln to 2336°F (1280°C). The glazes are mainly celadons with wax motifs and overglazes. Margaret Frith has been experimenting with copper red glazes, and both the Friths use copper reds in combination with heavy iron glazes and dark celadons.

The fountains are either self-circulating or designed to be set in ponds.

Self-circulating fountain by David Frith. Stoneware, celadon glaze with wax motif and over pigments and glaze trailing. H. 55 in. (1.4 m).

David Frith throwing a fountain bowl.

CAMERON WILLIAMS (AUSTRALIA)

Williams makes terracotta fountains which can be up to 93.6 in. (2.4 m) tall. They are assembled on site from many thrown pieces. First, a hollow metal pole containing the water pipeline is cemented into the ground and then a square brick base is laid. The fountain sections are threaded over the metal pole like a string of beads. Sometimes the work is filled with fiberglass to reinforce it. Most of the work is fired to 2102°F (1100°C), and is resistant to sub-zero temperatures.

Fountain with three bowls and a bird by Cameron Williams.

KATE MELLORS (UK)

Kate Mellors (see Chapter 5) includes fountains in her range of garden ornaments and planters. Some are wall mounted while others, such as the fountain illustrated, can be installed in a pond.

Smooth fountain by Kate Mellors, in stoneware with blue glaze.

CHAPTER 7

TABLES, BENCHES AND STOOLS

Seats and tables have been made from clay for centuries. West African and Far Eastern pottery have probably had the greatest influence on contemporary potters making garden furniture. While European furniture is often fixed in position, African or Chinese stools are smaller and portable. Portable seats like the barrel stools produced in Staffordshire by Brown-Westhead Moore in the 19th century, enjoyed a fashion in Victorian Britain and were used in conservatories. The designs were often very fanciful, such as a monkey and cushion seat produced by Minton in 1860, now in City of Stoke-on-Trent Museum.

There are many examples of decorated seating in Spain. The Catalan architect Antoni Gaudí used

Mosaic benches by Antoni Gaudí. Parc Güell, Barcelona, Spain.

LEFT: Earthenware barrel seat with yellow glaze by Brown-Westhead Moore 1862-1904.
Photo: Courtesy of City of Stoke-on-Trent Museum.

ceramic tiles to make mosaic benches in the Parc Güell in Barcelona, while colorful tiled seats can be seen in many town parks in Spain, particularly in the south.

Most of the potters in this chapter make garden furniture in addition to other items. Their work is often made of stoneware which is glazed and high fired. An exception is the work of Gwen Heeney who uses brick to make sculptural benches. These are of such a large scale and mass that Heeney collaborates with brick manufacturers to complete her projects. The works are fixed installations and stand in contrast to the portable stools and tables made by other potters featured in this chapter.

The influence of Nigerian clay furniture can be seen most directly in the stools and tables made by Chris Lewis and Kate Mellors.

Ceramic bench in a park in Cadiz, Spain.
Photo: Robin Parrish.

CHRIS LEWIS (UK)

While Chris Lewis thrives on the challenge of throwing very large pots, he also likes the slower and more demanding discipline of handbuilding. His sculptural garden seats are handbuilt and reflect his interest in West African wood carving, pots and buildings. He is also influenced by Oceanic wood carving, pre-Columbian Inca and Chancay pottery from Peru and Mimbres pots from the American Southwest. Lewis always starts with the object or shape that he wants to make rather than the garden space. He likes the objects that he produces to have a practical purpose rather than to be purely sculptural.

Techniques

Lewis makes a range of large thrown pots as well as handbuilt furniture or sculptures. The same clay forms the basis of both types of work, but the throwing body is mixed 50:50 with Craft Crank

Handbuilt sculptural seat by Chris Lewis. Stoneware with incised decoration.

clay for the larger pieces. The principal clay body is bought in powder form and mixed in a concrete-lined pit in the ground. The recipe is:

Hyplas 71	6
Hymod AT	3
Molochite 80s mesh	1

This is mixed with water, put through a large pugmill twice, then stored. It is pugged again immediately before use. Most garden work is unglazed but, as it is fired in a wood kiln, it becomes thinly glazed with fly ash from the fire boxes. Some pots are decorated with slips.

The kiln has two chambers. The first chamber is 125 cu. ft. (3.5 m^3) and the second is 100 cu. ft. (2.8 m^3) in capacity. The kiln is warmed for a day prior to firing and the firing itself takes 18 to 20 hours to reach stoneware temperature.

Pots and other pieces which are too heavy to be lifted by one person are lifted by two or three people using straps secured like belts under the belly of a pot. Sometimes pieces are moved by cradling them in blankets which are lifted by the four corners, while for other pieces a trolley is the best option.

Stoneware seat with curved arm rests by Chris Lewis.

KATE MELLORS (UK)

Mellors makes stools and tables as part of her garden range. Most of her other work is undecorated and relies on form for its ornamental qualities. Stools and tables, however, are decorated with incised geometrical patterns. Mellors says that the shapes and patterns of African pots inspired her to work in this way – her stools are based on African drum shapes. The seats of the stools are pierced to allow rain water to drain away.

Table and stools by Kate Mellors. Stoneware with incised decoration and piercing.

Karin Hessenberg (UK)

A stool was one of the first pieces I made when I started making handbuilt pots. The shape was derived from carved wooden window frames and eaves I had seen in Indian and Nepalese temples and palaces. The stools and tables are constructed using the slab techniques described in Chapter 5.

The stool has a dual purpose and can serve as a base for a plant pot or a sculpture, as well as a seat.

Stoneware stool, Kulu Pattern, blue ash glaze by Karin Hessenberg. H. 14 in. (37 cm).

Hans and Birgitte Börjeson (Denmark)

The Börjesons both worked with Harry and May Davis in England and were influenced by the work and ideas of Lucie Rie and Bernard Leach. They originally made thrown, reduced stoneware domestic pottery using a range of dark tenmoku glazes based on Swedish granite, which they fired in an oil-fueled kiln. They built their first salt kiln in the early 1980s and began working with different clay bodies which produced new, lighter colors. It was during this time that they began taking commissions for salt-glazed paving blocks,

Blue salt-glazed bench by Hans and Birgitte Börjeson.

benches and columns. These are made from hollow modules which can be assembled and permanently installed using concrete and mortaring techniques. The size of their work grew in response to these demands and Hans Börjeson's early training in industrial ceramics proved useful in the large architectural commissions they have undertaken. Hans usually constructs the forms while Birgitte does the decoration.

Hans Börjeson filling fired bench seat modules with concrete and inserting metal ties to fix them to the legs. He is using a ladder laid on trestles as a support and each piece is carefully numbered.

Hans Börjeson at work next to a set of modules drying on boards. The modules are braced with internal struts of clay which strengthen the structure and prevent warping.

GWEN HEENEY (UK)

Gwen Heeney studied ceramics at Bristol Polytechnic and then set up a business making terracotta garden pots. Although it was successful she became increasingly disillusioned with the lifestyle of the country potter after more than ten years of pressing out ornamental pots. She knew that she wanted to move into making commissions and in 1987 gained a place at the Royal College of Art to study for an MA in Ceramics.

Her student work experience placement at Hathernware Ceramics changed the direction of her work. At Hathernware she was impressed with the sophisticated technology that brick and architectural ceramic factories had at their disposal. Part of her research was to find out how artists might be accommodated in brick factories to work on unusual commissions. She became convinced that working with industry was the way for her to carry out her commissions.

Heeney has always wanted her art to communicate directly with people, and public commissions are an ideal means of achieving this aim. When designing a sculpture for a specific location, Heeney looks at both the physical space and its history. Most of her commissions have been for locations in Wales and she has drawn much of her imagery from Celtic mythology. She feels that many of the stories in these legends have relevance today and that people can relate to the emotions and the drama of the stories.

Techniques

When Heeney takes on a commission she visits the site and makes notes and drawings for her ideas. The next step is to make a model in her studio. She then shows her ideas to brick manufacturers to find out whether they are interested in the project.

Once an arrangement has been reached, she works in the factory using the clay blocks which are directly extruded on the production line. The blocks are covered with machine oil from the extruder and this helps their separation at the end

Carved brick seat in the form of a boar by Gwen Heeney. Caer Fawr Wood, Powys.

of the making process. Heeney piles up the large blocks of wet clay to make a mound a bit larger than the final sculpture, allowing excess for carving. The wet blocks are kept in place by suction.

Heeney uses a sharp gardening spade to rough out the shape of the sculpture. Once she has the rough shape she begins to carve with a large loop tool which cuts through the brick clay very rapidly. She continues carving with smaller, sharper loop tools. The final stage can be painstaking and lengthy, depending on the level of finish she requires.

At the end of the carving the sculpture has a perfectly smooth surface, and the lines between the blocks begin to appear as it dries. At this stage the blocks are easily dislodged. Once dry, the sculpture must be dismantled for firing. It is broken down into all of its components, which each have to be lettered and numbered. This prevents them being lost and ensures that the fired sculpture is correctly reassembled.

The fired brick blocks are mortared together to rebuild the form, which only Heeney and the factory staff will have seen when it was still wet and perfectly smooth. Heeney feels that this is an important element of the sculptural process. Her seats are both sculptural and architectural as well as being functional.

BELOW: Carved brick bench, 'Taliesin' by Gwen Heeney. Llanfair Caereinion Leisure Centre.

WILL LEVI MARSHALL (UK)

Levi Marshall (see Chapter 1) makes thrown stools as well as planters and jardinières.

ABOVE: Stoneware stool with colored glazes and geometrical patterns by Will Levi Marshall.

CHAPTER 8

ARCHITECTURAL FEATURES

While it is possible to make a clear distinction between garden ceramics such as planters or sundials, and architectural ceramics such as bricks and roof tiles, there is an area where they overlap. Some artists are making built structures for gardens such as archways and pillars, or substantial brick sculptures which can serve as seating. It is not only freestanding forms which are architectural. There is also a tradition of using murals or tiled paving to decorate gardens, particularly in Spain and Portugal.

Of the potters who have made freestanding constructed pieces, Gwen Heeney's work is on the largest scale and is more appropriate for landscapes than for small private gardens. Rosemary Metz and Su Lupasco have both made garden arches which are constructed from hollow sculpted modules.

Many potters produce murals or tiling for exterior walls or courtyard paving. The murals may be single panels or a set of interlocking pieces or tiles. They are often one-off pieces specially commissioned, as in the case of John Cliff. Other potters, such as Margery Clinton and Maggie Angus Berkowitz, who are both known for their tiles, produce work for both interior and outdoor locations.

Decorative ceramic wall and seat depicting Don Quijote, in Plaza de España, Seville, Spain.
Photo: Robin Parrish.

95

ROSEMARY METZ (UK)

Rosemary Metz is known for her plinth and lintel archways. She regards gardens as places for escape, contemplation and relaxation and she makes narrative pieces which fit into this context. Stories of the Creation myth from various cultures are a favorite subject for her visual imagery. These may be represented figuratively or in abstract form. As the narrative is important, text is sometimes incorporated into the images. She feels that the way in which ceramics are displayed in museums influences our perception of them, and may alter our attitudes to the objects. For example, an ordinary, utilitarian pot may acquire a special status if displayed as a precious object.

Her plinth and lintel archways provide a symbolic form as well as having large flat surfaces on which to carve and model reliefs, and paint pictorial images. The 'Archway with Nine Muses' illustrates the way in which Metz fuses these aspects in a single piece. Several sources of imagery are drawn together for the theme of this archway, which is about the nature of artistic creativity. The structure relates to the plinth and lintel style of building found in pre-Roman buildings in the Mediterranean region. The visual references in the decoration of the arch reflect past attitudes to creativity which differ from contemporary views.

The main story of the piece is in the lintel which depicts the Muses of Greek mythology. The legend of a singing competition between the nine victorious true Muses and the nine false Muses is written on the back of the arch using various relief lettering techniques. The message of the myth is the victory of creative integrity over imitation and falsification. The images on the plinth section refer to the woodcut, 'Melancholia', by Albrecht Dürer. The main figure represents melancholy, a mood which was considered necessary for artistic creativity in Dürer's time.

Techniques

Metz uses coils or rolled slabs to construct her work. The clay is usually Potclays Craft Crank and the slabs are rolled out using a converted washing mangle. Large pieces such as the archway are made from modular sections which she is able to lift and fire separately before they are assembled to make the complete form. When making a work of this size (93.5 x 58.5 in./2.4 x 1.5 m) several factors have to be considered. These include the strength and suitability of the clay body, the ability of the structure to stand up in all

'Archway with Nine Muses' by Rosemary Metz.

Porcelain letters carved by Rosemary Metz for stamping text into clay slabs for the 'Archway with Nine Muses'.

weather conditions, and the need for firm foundations to ensure the stability of the piece.

The sections for the archway are gently tapered towards the top, with the base pieces being the widest and strongest. The plinth blocks are shorter nearer the top. Each block has interlocking lip sections which are designed to accommodate stainless steel nuts and bolts. Stainless steel and greasing of the fastenings are essential to prevent rusting, which could make dismantling the piece very difficult.

All the pieces for the archway were raw glazed, a technique which is practical for large pieces as they need only to be fired once. Metz finds that the color response with oxides is better

Section of 'Archway with Nine Muses' showing interlocking lips and stainless steel nuts and bolts.

with raw glazing, and she uses strontium carbonate which adds stability to the glaze.

Strontium Base Glaze, 2156°–2228°F (1180°–1220°C)

Cornish stone	40
Strontium carbonate	35
Zinc oxide	4
Titanium oxide	4
Tin oxide	4
China clay	13
Lithium carbonate	4
Coloring oxides	2

To write the story of the Muses on the reverse side of the archway, Metz had to devise a way of creating text in relief. She chose to use lettering stamps and, as these were difficult to find ready-made, she carved her own upper case letters from porcelain. The smooth porcelain was the most suitable clay for this kind of detailed work and her letter stamps were fired to high earthenware temperature before being used. Other letters were obtained from a supplier of hot metal type.

To install the work, Metz ensures that the ground is leveled before laying a heavy paving slab as a base. If possible, turf is removed and the space leveled with builders' grit and sand before laying the slab and erecting the sculpture. The sections are screwed together using stainless steel nuts and bolts as illustrated.

The work is fired to high enough temperature to resist the effects of weather and Metz treats it with a transparent liquid water sealant used for waterproofing brickwork.

Su Lupasco (UK)

Su Lupasco (also see Chapter 5) makes large architectural pieces for the garden as well as producing sundials and birdbaths. She makes finials and window surrounds and she has built a 117 in. (3 m) arch which is installed in a garden. The arch comprises pillar sections, curved arch pieces and decorative modeling mounted on internal metal supports, and is assembled in such a way that it could be dismantled if necessary.

Arch, ceramic and mixed media by Su Lupasco, H. 113 in. (2.9 m).

Hans and Birgitte Börjeson (Denmark)

Hans and Birgitte Börjeson, who make salt-glazed benches and decorative paving blocks, also make sculptural columns for gardens. The columns can be installed as a feature in the garden or be part of a porch or veranda. The Börjesons' decorative columns are built of cylindrical modules which can be stacked up and mortared together like bricks. They require laying on a firm base and the level needs to be checked as the columns are constructed.

It is notable that potters in the United Kingdom rarely collaborate with industry, whereas this practice is fairly common in Scandinavia. This may be due to the different attitudes in Scandinavian Art School courses, where artists are encouraged to design for industry.

Decorated salt-glazed pillar, constructed from cylindrical sections by Hans and Birgitte Börjeson.

Hans and Birgitte Börjeson installing pillars.

An internal supporting rod is fixed into the ground and the first section of the pillar is lowered over this, leveled and cemented in position.

The pillar is mortared together and filled with concrete.

Hans Börjeson checks the level of a pair of pillars.

A pillar installed in the porch of a house.

GWEN HEENEY (UK)

Heeney's biggest project was the 'Mythical Beast' which she made for Garden Festival Wales in 1992. Constructed entirely of carved brick, the 'Mythical Beast' was also conceived as a garden to be planted, so spaces were left in its back for flowerbeds. This involved collaboration with a plant nursery and builders as well as the brickmakers, Ibstock of Bristol. As the Beast was so large, Heeney had to provide technical drawings as well as a scale model. Some shapes were worked out on the computers at Ibstock and the staff made special molds and machinery for some parts of the Beast, which was nicknamed Billy. The sculpture was dismantled, fired and the pieces delivered to the festival site at Ebbw Vale where the sculpture was rebuilt and then planted.

Part of the 'Mythical Beast' at Ebbw Vale by Gwen Heeney.

Tail of the 'Mythical Beast' being used as seats and flowerbeds.

GORDON BROADHURST (UK)

Gordon Broadhurst makes large-scale work only for commission, which means that he does not produce runs of similar forms or even use the same technical process every time. Sometimes he builds pieces from modules which are press molded using a heavy grogged clay body, while other work is slip cast using a smooth clay.

One particular commission required a set of large interlocking terracotta blocks to make a fountain. Broadhurst devised a method of making the blocks from slip cast modules. Slip casting is a process which requires a fine-bodied clay, and slip cast forms usually have thin walls so they are not normally substantial enough to be used in building work. Broadhurst solved this problem by filling his hollow fired modules with concrete and a waterproofing additive. This converted them into heavy solid blocks and also reduced the risk of frost damage.

Techniques

Gordon Broadhurst used the technique of sledging plaster to make the models for his slip cast blocks. Sledging is a technique where a template is drawn through soft, slow-setting plaster of Paris. The plaster shape is allowed to set hard and it can then be used on its own or joined to other sledged shapes to make a more complex form for producing a mold. This technique has been used for many centuries by decorative plasterers in the building industry. Moldings and covings were produced by the craftsman running a profile through a length of soft plaster. The plaster was either laid in position or sledged on a bench to make a piece for fixing later. There are three basic ways in which

Fountain by Gordon Broadhurst. Slip cast in red earthenware and fired to 2048°F. H. 10 in. (25 cm) x W. 58.5 in. (150cm).

Fig. a: Sledging a simple profile in a straight line using the edge of the work bench as a guide.

Fig. b: Sledging a shape using a profile across two directions. The sledge guide uses the top surface of the work bench.

Fig. c: Making a shape with a circular section by using a sledge attached to a pivot in the center of the heap of plaster.

Fig. d: Cross-section of Gordon Broadhurst's fountain block divided into three simpler shapes; a, b, and c.

Fig. e: Templates Broadhurst made from the three simple shapes illustrated in fig. d.

Fig. f: Running a length of plaster with a sledge and profile.

Fig. g: How a plaster mold is constructed for slip casting a corner block for the fountain.

Fig. h: Mold sections for a straight side block for the fountain.

plaster can be sledged: in a straight line; by following a given shape; or around a central pivot.

For his fountain blocks Broadhurst used several different profiles to sledge shapes; these were then joined together to make the complete block form. First he decided on a cross-section for the whole block and drew it accurately on a sheet of paper. He divided the drawing of the cross-section into three simpler shapes, cut them out and transferred them on to 0.039 in. (1 mm) thick aluminium sheet. He then cut these templates out with a saw and finished off the edges with a file and emery paper.

In this method, each of the thin metal templates has to be supported firmly on two pieces of timber sheet, (plywood or thin chipboard) which are fixed together at right angles. The support is the sledge. One piece of the timber supports the template which is attached by means of a few small nuts and bolts, while the other piece forms a guide which is slid along the work bench to keep a straight line.

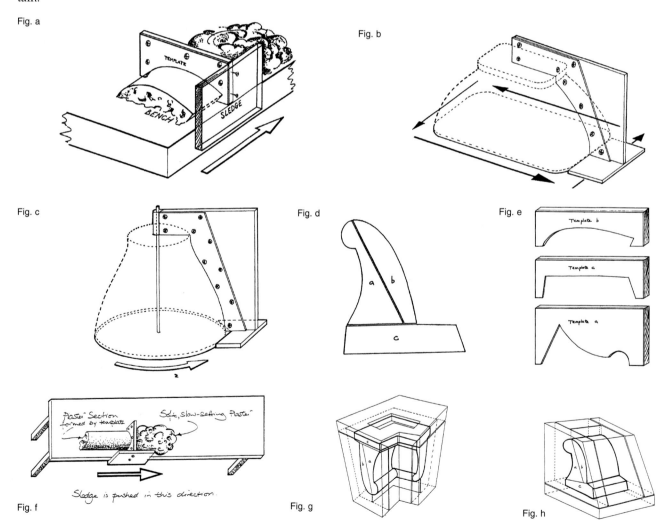

Fig. a

Fig. b

Fig. c

Fig. d

Fig. e

Fig. f

Fig. g

Fig. h

The work bench for sledging the plaster has to have a straight edge and be smooth and impervious to water. This is essential for the plaster moldings to be true and to allow the set shapes to be removed easily. Plastic-coated chipboard or a sheet of acrylic polycarbonate are ideal materials for this purpose and can be used as a temporary surface when laid on a conventional wood bench.

Broadhurst uses slow-setting plaster for sledging his forms. This can be bought with the retardant already incorporated, or a small amount of tri-sodium citrate can be added to the water before adding the plaster of Paris. A few trials with increasing amounts of tri-sodium citrate will demonstrate how the working time of the plaster can be extended. After the retardant has been added to the water, Broadhurst adds the plaster, lets it slake and then mixes it. When the plaster has thickened enough to stand in soft piles, he lays it on the work bench at one side of the sledge. Then he holds the sledge firmly against the front edge of the work bench and runs the length of the plaster by pushing it in one direction. The plaster section is formed through the gap in the profile and more soft plaster can be added as needed.

He continues sledging and adding plaster until he has the required length of plaster and the surface is smooth. The plaster of Paris takes 45 to 60 minutes to set hard, then he carefully removes the section from the bench. He makes a new section by repeating the sledging process with a different template. He joins the plaster sections with a thin mixture of the slow-setting plaster.

When the sections are firmly stuck, he cuts them into shape with a cross-cut saw which he finds perfect for cutting wet plaster, as the large off-set teeth do not clog up or cause the saw blade to bind. When the shapes are finished, he prepares them with a sealant such as soft soap to make plaster molds suitable for slip casting or press molding. His molds are thick-walled to allow a number of casts or pressings to be made without the mold becoming saturated.

Broadhurst's slip cast blocks are an example of an industrial technique being applied to individual studio work.

In a completely different way, John Cliff also relied on industrial production, for the large mosaics he made for a public art commission.

JOHN CLIFF (AUSTRALIA)

John Cliff had to develop new ways of working when he undertook several large commissions after an earthquake hit the town of Hamilton. One of these commissions was for large planters for the main shopping precinct, Beaumont Street, also known as Eats Street because of its many different ethnic restaurants.

Cliff's Commission

The idea for fractured tile mosaic planters came about after another artist had been commissioned to produce mosaic work for the pavements and it was decided to continue the theme with the planters. Cliff admired the work of Antoni Gaudí and saw the project as an opportunity to try making mosaics himself. He bought large ready-made concrete planters, and made his own thrown majolica-decorated plates and hand-painted majolica tiles. Using these and some commercially available wall tiles, he applied mosaics to the sides of the planters. The row of tiles at the top and the plates, which were applied as whole pieces, conveyed the imagery associated with the

Mosaic planter by John Cliff in Beaumont Street, Hamilton, Australia. 20 x 30 x 30 in. (51 x 75 x 75 cm).

Detail of one of John Cliff's mosaic planters.

MARGERY CLINTON (UK)

Margery Clinton studied painting at Glasgow School of Art and then did an MA at the Royal College of Art where she began research into reduction luster glazes. She has become involved with a number of architectural projects and is particularly interested in tiles, which she fires with reduction luster glazes.

Tiled sign by Margery Clinton for the Macaulay Gallery, Stenton, Scotland

diverse cultural communities of Hamilton. To date, 26 planters have been placed in Eats Street.

When he received the commission his own studio was too small, had poor access and no lifting equipment. He had to rent a larger space and found premises at the rear of a retail tile shop. This gave him access to a forklift, a pallet jack and also provided him with tiles for his mosaics. The concrete planters (which weigh 550 lb./250 kg when they are tiled) came in on pallets which were raised on to concrete blocks for a comfortable working height. When finished they went out on pallets via the forklift and after being planted, they were installed in the street by the local council.

Commercially made blank tiles are often used by artist potters for decorating. Both Margery Clinton and Maggie Berkowitz use industrial blanks where a particular project or commission requires them.

Detail of mosaic seat by Antoni Gaudí (see page 87).

Her commissions have included a tiled wall sign for the Macaulay Gallery in Stenton, Scotland, and a tiled wall fountain. The sign for the Macaulay Gallery is made of handbuilt vitreous terracotta tiles with inglaze reduction lusters.

The wall fountain is built into a tiled panel which Clinton made from industrial earthenware bisque tiles, which she decorated with screen-printed glazes and inglaze reduction lusters. The basin and cascade of the fountain are constructed from thrown and altered T-Material. The blackbird which forms the spout is made of vitreous terracotta with inglaze reduction luster on the eyes and beak. For a quiet flow, a chain hanging from a hook in the bird's beak channels the water below the surface of the water in the basin.

Reduction luster tiled fountain with blackbird spout by Margery Clinton.

MAGGIE ANGUS BERKOWITZ (UK)

Maggie Berkowitz specializes in tiles and uses them to make pictures in glaze. Berkowitz usually works to commission and her tiles can be set in both interior or open-air settings. She works on industrially produced blanks and floor tiles using a range of slips, oxides and earthenware glazes to create her designs and pictures. The tiles in the illustration are in an open courtyard in a primary school near her home in the Lake District.

Earthenware tiles in school courtyard, Cumbria, by Maggie Angus Berkowitz.

MARGARET AND DAVID FRITH (UK)

Margaret Frith has spent the past few years developing a translucent porcelain clay body and glazes which fit this clay. She carves her porcelain jars and bowls with floral designs and glazes them with a pale blue celadon glaze.

Frith is currently experimenting with copper red glazes and both she and David Frith use them in combination with glazes rich in iron to produce shades of deep purple, orange and red. They use these glazes on large murals which are composed of interlocking sections. The whole area of the mural is decorated with poured, painted and trailed glazes, often applied over a white base glaze. Margaret Frith uses wax to paint an initial design, or masks selected areas before applying more layers of glaze.

Wall piece, 'Shaped Blocks', by Margaret Frith. Poured copper red glazes on stoneware. Reduction fired to 2336°F (1280°C). H. 29 in. (75 cm).

Margaret Frith glazing a mural.

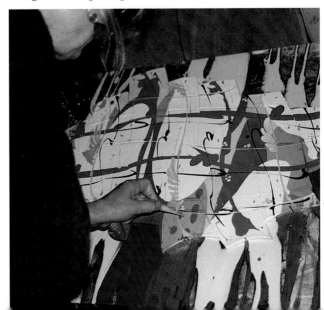

ABOVE: 'Flames' mural by David Frith.

BELOW RIGHT: Stoneware relief by Ali Jeffery (see Chapter 10) on a wall in a London garden.

BELOW LEFT: David Frith extruding sheets of clay which are joined to make the base for the tile murals.

CHAPTER 9

FIGURATIVE SCULPTURE

Sculpture for gardens has a long history. The Romans placed statues in the avenues and colonnades of palace or temple gardens and this tradition persisted in European gardens. The nobility and the wealthy in Europe commissioned the best sculptors of their time to make statues for their gardens.

Garden statuary was often derived from classical mythology and it was intended to have symbolic meaning or significance in the garden, although much of this symbolism has been forgotten today. The statues would be placed at key points, such as the end of an avenue or vista, and they would be lifesize or larger.

In the mid 18th century the rococo style became fashionable. The solemnity of the classical figure was replaced with amusing and whimsical sculptures of rustic characters such as gardeners, shepherdesses, musicians, dwarves and animals. Up until this period statues were usually made of materials such as stone, bronze or painted lead.

Roman sculptures in the Canopus at Hadrian's Villa in Tivoli, Italy.

The most notable early ceramic figures in Britain appeared at about this time. They were made to look like stone and were marketed as artificial stone. The best known was Coade Stone and the recipe was a carefully guarded secret, but it is known to have been a mixture of a white clay, ground glass, grog, flint and sand. It was fired for about four days in gas kilns at a fairly high temperature until vitrified. Coade Stone was a success because, unlike the soft English sandstones or Italian marbles, it did not weather or become covered with excessive growths of lichen. It was an attractive stony beige color which looked very natural, and kept its color and the details of the modeling. It was used to make ornamental urns, architectural friezes and sculptures.

Coade Stone statues were press molded in sections, and the pieces joined on the inside. When the sculpture was stiff enough for the molds to be removed, the outside seams were carefully concealed with slip, and further details could be added to the figure. It was not long before companies such as Blashfield developed their own versions of artificial stone and, by the 19th century, Doulton of Lambeth was producing frost-resistant terracotta figures as part of their range of garden ornaments.

In Britain, the interest in sculptures for gardens declined under the influence of Capability Brown and the landscape movement. Statuary was revived for the suburban gardens which developed during the 19th century but statues were relatively small, with those made by Doulton being only about 35 in. (0.9 m) tall. The most popular ornaments for these gardens were sundials and birdbaths.

In recent years there has been a growing market for small figures, both human and animal. Garden centers sell a vast array of cast concrete nymphs, dogs, frogs, otters, owls and herons. These may be used as supports for birdbaths and sundials, or simply exist to decorate a pond or a patio. There are terracotta wall planters in the form of classical Greek heads and any number of garden gnomes. The origins of gnomes are obscure. They may derive from the grotesque or rococo figures of dwarves from early grand gardens, or they may have been figures from ancient folklore which were kept as talismans to ward off evil and bring luck to the household.

There is a great deal of interest today in outdoor ceramic sculpture but much of this sculpture is abstract. Figurative ceramic sculpture in Britain is aimed largely at the gallery market.

Some artists specialize in animal sculptures, often commissioned by wealthy clients, and so they continue a long tradition of animal statuary. Sally Arnup, Ian Gregory and Anne James make animals, while other artists, such as Patricia Volk, are more interested in the human figure.

'Summer' from a page of a 19th century Doulton of Lambeth catalogue.
Photo: Reproduced courtesy of the Museum of Royal Doulton.

SALLY ARNUP (UK)

Sally Arnup is one of Britain's leading animal sculptors and although she usually works in bronze, she occasionally makes animals in fired clay. Her ceramic pieces are often modeled solid on an armature. The sculptures are cut off the armature, hollowed out and rejoined before being fired to biscuit temperature. Arnup sprays her sculptures with either iron oxide or glaze and then fires them to 2336°F (1280°C), which makes them hard enough to withstand outdoor conditions.

Arnup's animals are portraits from life and she makes detailed observations and drawings before starting the modeling process. There is no stylisation or abstraction in her animals and every mark and gesture in the surface of the clay exists to bring out the character of the animal or bird.

'Bulldog Pup' by Sally Arnup.

IAN GREGORY (UK)

Ian Gregory was encouraged by the sculptor Liz Frink to use clay as a sculptural medium. In his work he seeks to combine sculptural forms with the effects of glazing and firing. His human figures and animals, which can be lifesize, are based on observations but are not intended to be exact portraits. He regards producing work for open spaces as a challenge, since the piece has to work from many different viewpoints and be compatible with its setting.

Techniques

Gregory makes his sculptures from grogged clay bodies which incorporate fillers such as paper pulp, nylon fiber, cotton fibers and crushed brick. These give the body strength and lightness, enabling him to build very large pieces which do not become too heavy to move easily. His preferred clay body is based on Potclays Y-Material

'Hound Dog' by Ian Gregory. 19 x 33 in. (48 x 86 cm). Raku slips and low salt firing.

with additions of fireclay, grog and sand. He either raku-fires his sculptures or salt-glazes them and some pieces are smoked. The raku pieces are not completely frostproof, so Gregory uses high-fired stoneware for large outdoor commissions. For some garden sculptures he uses a low-firing earthenware clay or a brick clay body which vitrifies at around 1976°–2012°F (1080°–1100°C) and this provides some resistance to frost. He advises customers to protect low fired raku from frost.

Gregory builds each sculpture on a fixed base and then constructs a fiber kiln around it. He has designed his own flat-pack fiber kiln for ease of transportation and storage. The sides and top of the flat-pack kiln comprise panels of ceramic fiber block, fixed to a backing support of sturdy metal weldmesh using ceramic buttons and nichrome wire. Extra insulation is provided by putting a sheet of radiator foil between the ceramic fiber and the weldmesh support. He then treats the ceramic fiber with 'Rigidizer', a form of colloidal silica, dye and wetting agent. The 'Rigidizer' forms a hard skin on the ceramic fiber which stiffens it and prevents it from degrading. He leaves the edges of the blocks untreated so that they will compress together when the supported panels are assembled to make the kiln.

Assembling the kiln is simple. The floor is made from bricks with a piece of ceramic fiber blanket laid on top and a 1 in. (2.5 cm) thick layer of sand is spread over the blanket. The unfired sculpture is placed on this floor and the walls of the kiln are constructed by standing the fiber and weldmesh panels on their edges and joining them together at the corners with jump lead clips. The roof panel is fixed on in the same way. Gregory leaves a hole near the bottom of the front panel for a burner port and there is another small hole near the top of the back panel which serves as a flue. A square of ceramic fiber blanket is used as a damper to open and close the hole as necessary. (See *Ceramic Review* 172, 1998.)

Salt-glazed torso by Ian Gregory, fired to 2372°F (1300°C). H. 45 in. (1.15 m).

ANNE JAMES (UK)

While Anne James is best known for her fine, lustered and smoked porcelain bottles and bowls, she made a group of bird sculptures especially for the Potters' Garden at the National Garden Festival in Wales. The birds proved very popular and she now makes them to order.

James' sculptures are in keeping with the tradition of animal and bird statues in gardens. She makes small bird forms such as doves, water birds, partridges and chickens from grogged stoneware clays such as Craft Crank or T-Material.

The shapes are slightly simplified but based on observations of the movements and physical characteristics of the different birds. The sculptures are partly press-molded and partly hand-built and modeled and James decorates them with slips and oxides. Depending on the colors she wishes to obtain, the birds are fired to stoneware temperature in either a gas or an electric kiln.

Stoneware hen by Anne James. H. 14 in. (36 cm).

KARIN HESSENBERG (UK)

One of the reasons I started making objects for gardens was a desire to work on a large scale. My figurative pieces came about as a result of teaching a modeling course in the 1980s. I had always enjoyed life sculpture when I was a student and I decided to make some heads myself. The 'Flower Man' and 'Flower Woman' were based on real heads and designed to contain flowers as part of their headdress.

The National Garden Festival of Wales provided me with an opportunity to make sculptures for the Potters' Garden. I made four heads representing the Four Elements and a lifesize 'Forest Man', inspired by Arcimboldo, the 16th century painter famous for his illusionistic heads composed of fruit, vegetables or flowers. The head of the 'Forest Man' is based on the only two known portraits of Arcimboldo, while the clothes are decorated with sprigs of pine needles and cones. I admire the work of the Russian sculptor, Sergei Konionkov (1874–1971), particularly his treatment of portraits, in which he uses the neck and shoulders to bring out the character of his subjects.

Techniques

The head sculptures were handbuilt from Craft Crank clay on a simple armature made of a wooden post with a wire balloon on top, fixed to a stand. I cut up a metal coat hanger to make the balloon. Clay was built up on the armature in lumps, with key points on the head being measured with callipers.

'Flower Man' stoneware with blue ash glaze by Karin Hessenberg. H. 22.6 in. (58 cm).
Photo: Robin Parrish.

Female head representing 'Water' (approximately lifesize) by Karin Hessenberg. Stoneware, blue ash glaze.
Photo: Robin Parrish.

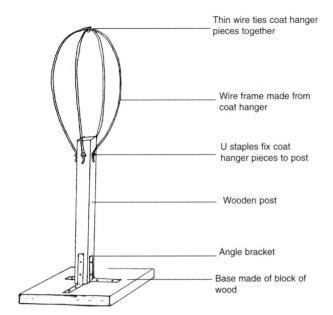

Thin wire ties coat hanger pieces together

Wire frame made from coat hanger

U staples fix coat hanger pieces to post

Wooden post

Angle bracket

Base made of block of wood

Balloon armature for sculpting heads.

After the bulk of the clay had been added to the armature, the shape of the head and face was modeled in greater detail, with regular checks on the measurements. Much of the modeling was done with large and small sculptors' spatulas and I used sharp wire loop tools to refine the surface and details.

When the head was leatherhard, I removed it from the armature by cutting off the top third which was lifted away. I scooped clay out of each half to leave a shell just over 1 in. (2.5 cm) thick and then lifted the larger half off the armature. The two hollow halves were rejoined by scoring, wetting and sealing the seam together with a coil. I stood the head upside down in a thick ring of clay to finish the bottom edge of the neck. The shoulders were made separately with thick coils of clay and roughly modeled. When both the head and shoulder sections were leatherhard and the neck stiff enough to support weight, they were joined and the modeling was completed.

The surface was finished off by pressing a small piece of damp hessian over it to remove tiny lumps before adding sprigs or other textured decoration. The heads were glazed and fired to stoneware. Techniques for modeling clay heads and figures are well-described in Bruno Lucchesi's book *Terracotta Sculpture*.

I made the 'Forest Man' from T-Material and built it up with thick coils starting from the feet. This took two weeks and the coils were purposely made thick to allow for carving and shaping

'Forest Man' (approximately lifesize) based on Arcimboldo by Karin Hessenberg. T-Material, unglazed and fired to stoneware at 2300°F (1260°C).

once the figure was leatherhard. The head was made on an armature as described above. I made biscuit molds for the sprigs by pressing pine cones and needles into pieces of soft clay.

When the figure was complete and leatherhard, I cut it into six sections which could be lifted into the kiln. I added a 2 in. (5 cm) coil to the underside of each section, except for the bottom one, to make a male end which fitted into the top of the section below. I designed the head and neck to fit into the collar, with a tab on the base of the neck to prevent the head from tipping out of position. The sections were fired separately to stoneware temperature without any glaze.

The sculpture is now installed in my garden, partly filled with gravel for stability, and the seams are sealed with putty.

Patricia Volk (UK)

Patricia Volk is a sculptor who became involved with heads and faces after seeing mime theater, in which the actors use only facial expression and gesture to convey emotion and meaning. Volk works figuratively, but retains only the minimum of detail required to convey the meaning of her sculptures. She tries to capture the pure structure of the head form. The work of Brancusi has had a great influence on her.

Although her heads are not portraits, Volk finds that during the slow process of modeling they develop their own personalities. The sculptures are fired to a high bisque temperature and then patinated with acrylics, varnishes and metallic pigments. Her use of color is inspired by ancient Egyptian artifacts, while the gold leaf is a direct reference to medieval icons.

Volk's sculptures are not all for gardens, although she is often asked to make work for an open-air setting.

She is quite explicit in linking her work with spiritual traditions of the past, when images of heads or figures held symbolic significance. Some of her head sculptures have slender, elongated faces which are poised on slim necks and shoulders and mounted on bases. These are often brightly colored and the expression of the face, and pose of the head, are intended to convey feelings. Volk seeks to create an enigmatic mood in her sculptures. The smooth, pure lines of her heads, with the emphasis on the eyes and lips, give some a pensive expression with a hint of sadness, while others look serene.

Other heads are rounded and lie in groups on the ground, like giant pebbles or boulders resembling a stone circle. These heads are similar but subtly different, like individuals in a crowd.

'Deity' is a group of rounded heads shaped and colored like pebbles on a Scottish beach, each head being about 23 in. (60 cm) in diameter. The group was inspired by the ancient Celtic tradition of putting carved heads into wells to discourage children from jumping in.

Techniques

Volk handbuilds her sculptures using either white grogged stoneware (CCST, from Commercial Clays) or white St Thomas clay for smaller, more detailed work. The CCST is similar to T-Material but contains less grog.

Some of the heads are coiled, but those for 'Deity' were press-molded in a very simple two part mold. Each head had the same basic shape, with very little detail, and Volk then modeled them so that each developed a unique character.

The coiled heads are first modeled and, on completion, Volk divides them up. She cuts heads from shoulders and fires them separately because of the restrictions of kiln size. After firing, she glues the parts together again with glazing sili-

'Slender Blue Head' by Patricia Volk at Hannah Peschar sculpture garden.
Photo: Hannah Peschar.

cone before applying the paint finish; the joins are completely invisible in the finished piece.

She fires her work very slowly in an electric kiln, taking about two days to reach 2120°F (1160°C). At this temperature, the clay is still slightly porous and so can absorb the first layer of acrylic paint. However, Volk does not paint the heads immediately, preferring to wait until she has decided which colors most suit their characters.

She builds up the colors over several days, often changing her mind, and acrylic paints give her the freedom to alter the colors and be spontaneous. The pieces are sometimes finished with gold, silver or copper pigments. The colors are often meant to be symbolic, with blue representing water, or brown meaning earth.

When fully dry, the sculptures are finished with a coat of mineral spirit-soluble acrylic (MSA) varnish containing UVLS (Ultra Violet Light filters and Stabilizers) which protect them from damage by sunlight and makes them waterproof. The MSA varnish is physically tougher than water-based acrylic varnish and, if necessary, can be removed with mineral spirits after it has dried.

Volk mounts some heads on Welsh slate using a flexible silicone sealant. Hollow pieces are mounted on rods and filled with expanding foam filler. Steel stands and support rods for the heads are made by a local blacksmith.

The glazing silicone she uses for gluing her work together is the same substance as the flexible silicone sealant used for mounting. It is Mildew Resistant Silicone Sealant, an industrial sealant used for bonding glass, porcelain, ceramic, sanitary ware and painted surfaces in buildings. It creates an airtight seal and is available from builders' merchants.

'Deity' by Patricia Volk at Hannah Peschar sculpture garden. *Photo: Hannah Peschar.*

JANE NORBURY (UK/ FRANCE)

Jane Norbury started making sculpture in clay when studying for her BA in ceramics. She was more interested in working on a large scale and exploring form than in the chemistry of glazes. Although she is best known for her handbuilt planters, she occasionally works on large-scale installations or performance pieces in collaboration with other artists or musicians. She feels that this is a link with ancient Greek gardens which were often performance spaces.

In 1990 Norbury made nine giant terracotta heads called 'Têtes Brulées', a musical installation conceived with the French composer Etienne Delmas. The heads stand on metal bases in groups and a continuous resonance of whispering sound and song emerges from their open mouths. 'Têtes Brulées' was first exhibited in a small formal garden which was on several levels surrounded by box hedges. Norbury enjoys the challenge of siting sculpture and she has learned a lot from working with street-theatre performers, who have to respond to a new space each time they perform.

'Têtes Brulées' and some smaller heads which Norbury has placed in her own garden are figurative. More abstract is a recent installation called 'RoTerre', a performance piece involving dancers and musicians who manipulate terracotta spheres of different sizes to produce musical sounds.

Both 'Têtes Brulées' and 'RoTerre' explore the resonating quality of hollow terracotta forms. They are containers of sound and are both designed to function in garden spaces.

Techniques

Norbury's sculptures are made of heavily grogged brick clays. She coiled the heads for 'Têtes Brulées', following model forms and full-size profiles drawn on her studio wall. She modeled the details using her fingers and pieces of wood.

'King and Queen' sculptures by Jane Norbury in her garden in France.
Photo: Robin Parrish.

'Têtes Brulées' by Jane Norbury.

Her kiln was far too small to accommodate the heads, so some were fired in a friend's wood kiln while a fiber kiln was constructed around the largest ones. Her work was fired to 1904°F (1040°C).

'Black Venus' by Mo Jupp.
Photo: Peter's Barn Gallery.

MO JUPP (UK)

Mo Jupp is a sculptor whose work occupies a position between the representational and the abstract. He studied ceramics at Camberwell School of Art and the Royal College of Art. It was during this period that he met Hans Coper, who was an extremely influential teacher. Although Coper was a thrower, he made sculptural forms and many of his former students went on to develop work unconnected with vessels. Jupp became a sculptor in clay and his 'Helmet Forms' were regarded as quite revolutionary when they were first exhibited in the early 1970s.

'Andromeda' by Mo Jupp at Peter's Barn Gallery.
Photo: Peter's Barn Gallery.

Jupp handbuilds his sculptures using any relevant techniques such as slab building, coiling and modeling. Some are constructed in stoneware, others in porcelain, and they may be colored with slips, stains, glazes, and gold or silver lusters.

For almost 20 years Mo Jupp has concentrated on sculpting the female form, ranging in size from tiny figures only a few inches high to tall lifesize females. Recently, he has made sculptures for open-air settings. Some of the sculptures, such as his 'Black Venus', have references to classical Greek and Roman sculptures.

His latest figures have become stylized icons of the female form. These icons or totems are tall, thin poles built up from cylindrical sections and only tiny, rudimentary breasts indicate their femininity.

There are many artists making figurative pieces in ceramics and I believe that increasing numbers of those who wish to work on a larger scale are likely to produce work for the open air. Hitherto, figurative ceramics for gardens have attracted much less attention than abstract ceramic sculpture. The latter comprises an enormous variety of work, from smaller gallery pieces to architectural installations. In the next chapter I look at the work of certain artists whose work focuses on aspects of landscape and gardens.

'Female Icon' by Mo Jupp installed in the grounds of Peter's Barn Gallery.

CHAPTER 10

ABSTRACT
SCULPTURE

The advent of abstract art in the 20th century has led to a great variety of sculpture for gardens and landscapes. Ceramics have followed the path of bronze and stone, and sculptural work in fired clay has been developed for open-air settings, often by scaling up work made for interiors.

The work of artists such as Ewen Henderson, Peter Hayes and Felicity Aylieff falls into this category. Other artists, such as Ali Jeffery and Jean Lowe, intended their work to be placed in garden and landscape settings from the outset and have organized their studios and working methods accordingly.

Many of these sculptors not only make pieces for landscape but derive their ideas from elements of landscape and the natural world. A garden or landscape is more than a setting for their work – it is integral to it.

'Pillow Rock' by Ewen Henderson

PETER HAYES (UK)

Hayes' raku sculptures, which can be as tall as 117 in. (3 m) have developed from his vessels and small sculptural forms which relate to the forms of bone knives, discs and heads. Characteristic shapes include flattened bottles with well-defined, angular shoulders and tiny necks: the pieces he calls 'Bow' forms which have a smooth disc engraved into the surface; and 'Keyhole' forms which have a peep-hole near the top. Many of his large pieces have the same formal elements as the 'Keyhole' and 'Bow' form pots.

Despite the monumental scale of Hayes' sculpture, it is fired using the raku method which is noted for the fragility of the fired clay. It is the surface qualities created by raku firing which fascinate him. Raku provides a means for him to express his interest in the structure of landscapes. Folds and cracks in the clay, and the subtle colors of raku, combined with smooth burnishing and polishing, give a sense of age and timelessness to his work. As they age and weather, cracks form an integral part of the evolution of his sculptures and Hayes has developed techniques to accelerate this process.

Some of the most dramatic colors in raku are produced using copper, and Hayes has had a long involvement with this metal. He has now almost abandoned glaze and instead uses pure copper metal laid into the surface of his sculptures. Copper reacts with water to produce greens and blues and he exploits this to create subtle color variations in his work. The idea for this technique of coppered white clay came from white marble statues which he saw in Italy, where brass pins in the statues had reacted with rain and produced green, blue and brownish streaks on the marble.

Techniques

All his large sculptures are made in modular sections handbuilt from laminated slabs of clay. The slabs are made from layers of different clays which are rolled out and compressed on a slab roller. Hayes starts with a robust clay body which he overlays with a smooth white body which can be ground and polished. The compressed, rolled sheet of laminated clay is cut into shaped slabs which are used to build the form.

The fine white clay is not an ideal raku body but Hayes uses it because a rough grog would interfere with the polishing process at a later stage. The lamination of the clays produces cracks and fissures which he regards as part of the surface character of the sculpture and he describes himself as an 'artist in crack management'. The fracture lines are part of the effect and, to add to this, they are inlaid with copper.

The pieces are raku fired in a top-hat kiln deep enough to hold a 47 in. (1.20 m) high section of a sculpture. The sculpture is wired up in a supporting

Water Sculpture by Peter Hayes in the Japanese Garden, Marlborough. Raku fired, ground and polished. H. 51 in. (1.3 m)

net of nichrome wire to prevent it falling apart during the rigors of firing. It is placed on the kiln floor and the top-hat kiln is lowered over the sculpture by means of a hoist and chain.

When the correct raku firing temperature has been reached, the top of the kiln is lifted away and a metal cylinder is lowered over the hot sculpture. Sawdust is tipped into the cylinder to smoke the sculpture and it is left to reduce overnight. When the firing and reduction have been completed, the smoking cylinder is lifted away and the sculpture is revealed, looking like a piece of coal – rough and blackened with occasional glints of metal.

The copper metal fuses into the clay during the firing, but colors only begin to appear after the surface has been ground and polished. All the roughness is ground away until the cracks appear as metallic lines flush with the whole surface of the piece.

The sculptures are then aged under water. Hayes lives and works beside the River Avon and leaves his sculptures in the river for several months. The river water and salts in the clay react

Peter Hayes' top-hat kiln being lowered over an unfired sculpture.

Top-hat kiln being fired. A smoking cylinder, attached by chains to the same gantry as the kiln, stands beside it.

Two standing forms and a round form by Peter Hayes. Exhibited by the Scottish Gallery at Greywalls, Gullane, Scotland.
Photo: Robin Parrish.

The smoking cylinder filled with hot sawdust, is quenched with water to cool it and put out the flames.

with the copper which bleeds into the clay, producing subtle greens and blues. Occasionally he reverses the process, ageing the pieces under water before he grinds them. All pieces are subjected to further treatment, as Hayes continues sanding and rubbing the surface. The work is then polished and waxed to give a smooth sheen which brings out the colors. Some pieces are aged with salt water, giving different effects. This is done by leaving them under the sea or standing them on the seashore for spray to react with the copper.

If the sculptures were left simply as raku-fired clay they would be too fragile to survive for very long, so they are reinforced with a 0.5 in. (1.27 cm) layer of fiberglass on the inside. In effect, the sculptures are a raku shell strengthened with fiberglass. When the sculptures are completed they are given a solid but slightly flexible core of plastic filler similar to car body filler. The filler can be mixed and pasted into the pieces of the sculpture and after a time, it sets. The largest sculptures are mounted on a steel sleeve tube over a rod cemented into the ground. The filler is inserted into the sections as the sculpture is installed. The seams between the sections of the sculpture are glued with a strong epoxy resin such as Araldite mixed with graphite.

Smoking cylinder being lifted away.

Peter Hayes brushes ash off the smoked raku fired sculpture.

Ewen Henderson (UK)

Where Peter Hayes' work can be likened to the geology of water erosion, Ewen Henderson's is similar to the geology of volcanoes where rocks are metamorphosed by fire. His abstract forms have mineral qualities produced from within the clay during firing. They are geological in a material way, and are conceptually linked with landscape. Henderson paints landscapes and tries to capture both the physical elements of a landscape and its mood. The paintings provide source material for the form and surface of his sculptures. His earlier work consists of vessel forms around which he worked in both a sculptural and painterly way, experimenting with surface textures and colors and pushing clay to its limits.

Henderson's sculptures can be for outdoor or indoor environments and sculpture for the garden is only one aspect of his work. Many pieces are installed in his own garden in North London.

Plants have grown in and around them and they have acquired an aged quality. Some have almost disappeared into the living plants and earth.

Techniques

Henderson's paintings and visual notes hang above the work bench in his studio. They are semi-abstract and have features of a landscape pared down to the essentials. He makes ceramic pigments which correspond to the colors in the paintings, and uses these to color his sculptures.

He uses a variety of handbuilding processes and has evolved his own technique of slab building,

A sculpture by Ewen Henderson is mounted on a brick base and is surrounded by plants in his London garden.

Sculpture with horn inclusion by Ewen Henderson.

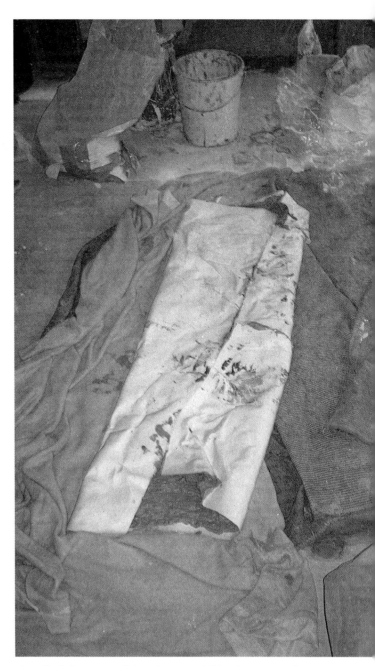

A soft slab wrapped in pigmented blotting paper lies on blankets on the floor of Henderson's studio.

in which thick slabs are built up from successive layers of clay slurry spread on a plastic sheet on the floor of the studio. As the slurry dries and stiffens, the slab can be lifted and manipulated into shape. This method enables him to transpose his paintings on to the clay using his monoprint process. First he paints previously mixed ceramic pigments on to a glass plate and then lifts the pigment by laying a large sheet of top quality blotting paper on to the painted glass. The blotting paper is then laid, pigment side up, on a plastic

sheet on top of a blanket spread on the floor. Then he pastes clay slurry, fiber, wire and any other chosen materials on to the blotting paper and the pigment colors are slowly absorbed into the clay as it dries. Henderson often incorporates nylon fiber, paper fiber, molochite, fiberglass and nichrome wire into the clay to give it strength and special texture. The slab ends up being about 2 in. (5 cm) thick and, as the clay stiffens, he lifts the slab on to its edge and maneuvers it into shape. The sculptures called 'Zigzag' are made in this

The stiffened slab, still wrapped in blotting paper, stands on its edge. Sheets of polythene protect the slab and help to control the speed of drying.

An experimental piece incorporating steel mesh stands on a work bench. Some of Henderson's paintings are pinned on the wall behind it.

way. They are 23 in. (60 cm) high, thick folded forms, some incorporating metal. The foldings correspond with folds in the blotting paper as the sculpture is manipulated on its edge.

When the piece is dry, the blotting paper is carefully peeled off so that it does not burn in the kiln and produce smoke, which would cause problems with his neighbors.

Henderson's studio and kilns are not large so he ensures that most of the work will fit the kilns and that he can lift it himself. Large pieces are made from modules which are assembled after firing. His tall sculptures consist of several pieces stacked on a metal post and joined with adhesive. These are carefully crafted so that the joints are virtually invisible. Where sculptures are installed outside, the high firing temperature provides weatherproofing. Eventually, however, they age and acquire growths of moss, due to the coarse and slightly porous character of the clay. Henderson likes this process and regards it as the natural evolution of the piece.

JIM ROBISON (USA/UK)

Although Jim Robison uses the techniques of a potter, his work is primarily sculpture. He became interested in making large outdoor ceramics while living in the USA, where he found that there was considerable interest in purchasing sculpture for private gardens.

He feels that his work looks best in natural surroundings, because he derives much of his inspiration from landscape. Although the forms are abstract, they often contain references to rocks, fossils and weathering processes.

Garden sculpture is just one aspect of his work, which includes architectural pieces such as wall-mounted reliefs. He also makes planters and fountains as well as smaller sculptural vases and plates.

Techniques

Robison's methods are those of a handbuilder and he uses heavily grogged clay such as Craft Crank to make large slabs which he rolls out using an adapted washing mangle as a roller. He textures the slabs by scoring, scratching and pressing in stamps and small found objects. The slabs are painted with slips and left to stiffen overnight. The next day the slabs are laid out on a large sheet of hardboard or wood and joined together to form even larger slabs for constructing sculptural forms. The large slab can, at this stage, be stood on its edge using the wood or hardboard as a support.

'Winter Figure' by Jim Robison next to a smaller untitled work at the Harley Gallery, Nottinghamshire.
Photo: Courtesy of The Harley Gallery.

Robison rolling out layered slabs on his converted mangle slab roller.
Photo: Nick Broomhead.

Stressed slab edges created by mutiple rolling.
Photo: Nick Broomhead.

Decorating a slab with porcelain slip. Robison uses a piece of net and a comb made from a toothed rubber kidney to create two different textures.
Photo: Nick Broomhead.

A single large slab is made up of a number of smaller ones joined together. Robison uses a support of hardboard and cloth which acts like a mold while he joins the slabs together. A matching large slab is made in a second hardboard mold placed at the end of the first mold to form the other side of the sculpture. When leatherhard and stiff enough, the two large slabs are raised to a vertical position and joined to form the sculpture. The slab in this picture is about 39.4 in. (1 m) long.
Photo: Nick Broomhead.

A second large slab, similarly supported on its edge, can then be joined to the first slab. The hardboard supports remain until the work is leatherhard and able to stand on its own. Robison continues working on the surface by modeling, pressing in stamps, sgraffito, and painting with porcelain slips.

It takes several weeks for the work to dry, after which it is raw-glazed and fired once. He applies glazes in layers with a spray gun, using as many as five different glazes, often with a high ash content. He controls the glazing process to create light and dark areas, starting with dark colors and adding successive layers of lighter colors. Pale areas are created by masking them against darker glazes or by gently rubbing away the dark colors in selected places before applying a layer of a lighter glaze. As most of the glazes are translucent, darker colors enrich the surface while underlying areas of white porcelain slip show through to provide contrast.

Robison's largest sculptures are made from big sections which can be bolted together at the finished stage. The individual sections are usually designed to be lifted single-handed, but very heavy pieces require help for lifting and loading into the kiln.

His work is reduction fired to vitrification at 2300°–2336°F (1260°–1280°C) in a brick-lined gas kiln. The first stages are slow, with warming overnight to just over 212°F (100°C) to ensure complete drying of the work. Then the kiln temperature is raised slowly through the early and middle stages of firing to avoid steam blowouts and carbon trapping. This helps prevent any bloating at later stages. Reduction is started at about 1864°F (1018°C) and continued until the end of the firing. The total cycle takes approximately 24 hours and at the end of the firing, Robison leaves the flue damper open for about 30 minutes to cool the kiln rapidly to around 1832°F (1000°C). This procedure seems to have no ill effects and saves about 12 hours of cooling time. The damper is then closed and the rest of the cooling takes about 30 hours. A fiber kiln would require less time to cool.

The high firing ensures that Robison's work is frostproof. The sculptures are also carefully designed for effective drainage, with holes in the base and shapes which allow the water to run off.

JEAN LOWE (UK)

Jean Lowe draws on landscape as a source of inspiration for her work, but in a different way from Ewen Henderson or Jim Robison. She lives beside the River Medway estuary in Kent, and the eroded forms of the pebbles and flints she finds on the tidal shore are echoed in the forms of her sculpture. The smooth, round pebbles and the craggy pieces of flint provide the basis for the forms she makes. The dark glassy insides of broken flints and their creamy, chalky surfaces influence her use of color and texture. She also draws inspiration from the shifting light and the cloudscapes over the river.

The sculptures are large abstract pieces which are not intended to be functional, although birds often bathe in the water-filled hollows. Her largest pieces are 36–48 in. (90–120 cm) high and 24–28 in. (60–70 cm) in diameter, and are inspired by rock forms. They are craggy and have titles such as 'Rock Pool' or 'Boulder'. Lowe also makes wide, shallow 'Pebble' forms which are smooth and quiet; and these can be up to 32 in. (80 cm) wide by 12 in. (30 cm) high. Most of the 'Pebbles' and some of the 'Boulders' have hollows in them, which will hold rainwater.

Lowe's sculpture is close to its sources and it is not her intention to move too far from the natural origins of the forms. Her work is abstract in the way she simplifies and distorts her forms. She aims to make objects which enhance their setting and induce a sense of calm contemplation and pleasure.

Lowe is a handbuilder whose method is coiling. She believes that her largest sculptures, which weigh up to 132 lb. (60 kg) after firing, probably represent the technical limit achievable for a single monolithic piece made by coiling. This is partly due to the problems of heat transfer and dispersion of stress which would arise in a larger piece, and partly due to the problems of moving and loading very heavy raw pieces into a kiln. Jean Lowe chose to work in a communal studio, knowing she needed access to a large kiln and helpers for lifting. Her methods of handling such large pieces are illustrated and described in 'Practical Considerations'.

OPPOSITE: 'Pebble LVII' by Jean Lowe 19 x 21 x 16 in. (56 x 62 x 48 cm).

Techniques

Lowe uses Craft Crank clay for most of her work, except for white 'pebbles', for which she uses T-Material. Although she uses slightly different methods for her two main groups of forms, Lowe coils them all as completely closed forms. This is why she calls her sculptures 'double-skinned' or 'double-walled'. A small hole is drilled in a discreet position near the bottom to let out air during firing.

For large craggy pieces she first makes small models providing the basis of the idea which is further developed as she builds the sculpture. She starts by rolling out a flat pad of clay 24–30 in. (60–90 cm) in diameter and then builds up with thick coils which she rakes upwards using wooden ribs and her fingers. This process thins the coils to give a strong but slender wall. Bulging forms are reinforced with vertically aligned coils on the inside rather like the ribs of a boat's hull.

To make pebble forms, Lowe begins with a small circle of clay and builds up coils to form what will be the upper part of the piece with its characteristic hollow. When this part is dry enough to handle she places a sponge block and a board on top of the form. She then turns it over to continue work on what will eventually be the underside of the finished piece. The thickness of the 'double-skin' walls is typically between 0.58–0.78 in. (15–20 mm).

All the sculptural work is dried very slowly for up to two months to avoid cracking. When the work is leatherhard Lowe applies many layers of slips. The slips are painted on and scraped back, then more layers are added and scraped and sponged away to give mineral qualities of color and texture. For the large 'Boulder' and 'Rock Pool'

pieces, she first brushes on slips colored with oxides. These are followed by slips of different colors which are sponged on to produce an effect like the ripple of water passing over stone. The rhythm of the marks follows the form of the piece.

The sculptures are bisque-fired to 1832°F (1000°C), and a dry matt glaze is sponged on while the work is still on the kiln shelf. The work is fired to 2300° or 2336°F (1260° or 1280°C), in either oxidation or reduction, depending on the effects Lowe wishes to achieve. Firing of the work is very slow and the biggest pieces are given a 24-hour period of preheating or 'toasting' before the bisque firing. Firing times are typically 15 hours for bisque and 12 hours for glaze firing.

She decorates the 'Pebble' forms in a similar way, but usually omits the sponged slips. Some of the Pebble forms are creamy white with a volcanic glaze to give the impression of a surface with small barnacles adhering to it.

Drawing showing stages in the construction of a 'Pebble' sculpture by Jean Lowe.

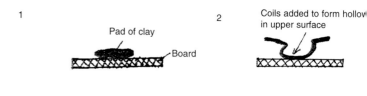

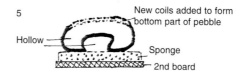

'Boulder VIII' by Jean Lowe. H. 48 in. (1.22 m).

No 1 Dry Glaze for Boulders, Rock Pools, Dark Pebbles.

China clay	30
Whiting	30
Lithium	10
Potash feldspar	10
Silicon carbide	3
Sinconium silicate	7

Creamy Matt Glaze

China clay	40
Whiting	31
Flint	18
Dolomite	7
Potash feldspar	4

For a volcanic effect, she first applies the Creamy Matt Glaze and then sponges the Dry Glaze on top.

In designing work for outside, Lowe ensures that it is frostproof by the high firing which prevents the absorption of moisture from the atmosphere or ground. She also takes care to avoid overhangs in the hollows of the work which might prevent the free expansion of water as it freezes, and turns to ice.

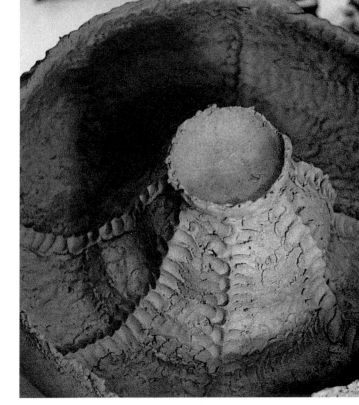

The inside of an upside-down 'Pebble' form showing the coil ribs Lowe makes to reinforce the walls.
All photos: Jola Spytkowska.

The round disc in the center is the pad of clay which Lowe used to start coiling at the start.

Lowe adding a coil to form the sides of the 'Pebble' form and gradually close in what will become the base of the sculpture.

Lowe raking up and thinning the clay she has just added to the sculpture.

FELICITY AYLIEFF (UK)

Felicity Aylieff was originally a potter rather than a sculptor, but she came to a point where she felt she had gone as far as she could with techniques and inspiration for her vessels. Her sculptures developed out of a desire to change scale and to work with a more specific environment in view. She now spends an equal amount of time working on large sculptures and small colored vessels. Her large-scale works in clay are both decorative and sculptural and she combines simplified natural forms and architectural detailing with a style derived from Indian sculpture.

She has developed her own clay body which has additions of glass and fired, colored porcelain. She describes this aggregate body as a ceramic terrazzo, which provides surface colors in the finished sculpture.

'Spiral' by Felicity Aylieff.

Styrofoam model of 'Spiral' form standing in a support and with clay walls built round areas to be cast for mold sections. By Felicity Aylieff.

Styrofoam model of 'Indian Leaf' sculpture by Felicity Aylieff.

Aylieff originally intended her sculptures to be placed in interior spaces such as foyers or entrances but clients found they were successful outside, so she now makes work for the open air.

Techniques

Her sculptures are made by press molding. The size and complexity of the forms require her to use sculptural techniques for making the model and molds rather than conventional pottery methods.

She starts by creating a small model of the piece in wax, plasticine or clay and then makes a full-size model out of Styrofoam (a dense form of polystyrene) before casting a multi-piece plaster mold to use as a press mold for the clay. The Styrofoam is lightweight and easy to maneuver and comes in sheets 4.4 in. (11 cm) thick. The full-size model is built up by stacking and glueing slices of Styrofoam together. The small model is marked out into segments proportional to the thickness of a Styrofoam sheet. A scaled up cross-section of each segment is drawn on to the

'Indian Leaf' sculpture by Felicity Aylieff. Mold pieces with the Styrofoam model in the background.

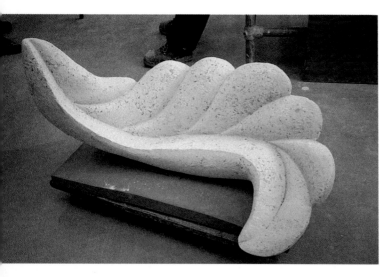

'Indian Leaf' sculpture after firing and before grinding and polishing.

Finished 'Indian Leaf' sculpture.

Styrofoam sheet, labeled, and cut out with a bandsaw. The pieces are stacked up in the correct order and glued together with an impact adhesive to make a full-size model of the form. She originally used Tretabond but now uses 3M polystyrene adhesive.

When Aylieff makes irregular forms, she makes a block of Styrofoam larger than the final piece and then carves directly into it with a handsaw. The details are refined with an electric carving knife and fine files, and sandpaper is used for the final smoothing of the surface. This is important, as the main texture of the sculpture is produced in the clay body with its aggregate inclusions. The foam model is sealed with two coats of emulsion paint and any blemishes are smoothed over with plasticine. (Safety precautions such as wearing masks and protective clothing should be taken as Styrofoam produces irritating dust and, if cut with a hot wire, poisonous fumes.)

The plaster molds are made in pieces that can be lifted by one person. Clay walls are constructed on the model around the mold section, on to which liquid plaster is then splashed. Thicker, stronger plaster reinforced with scrim is then pasted on to the splashed area to form a mold section approximately 1.2 in (3 cms) thick. When this section has set, the surface is tidied up, the clay wall is removed and the plaster sealed with soft soap. A new clay wall is built on to an adjacent area of the model and a further mold section cast in the same way. Aylieff makes natches (locating holes) on the walls before casting so that the mold sections fit accurately in position. She repeats the casting until all sections of the mold have been cast.

The complete mold, which may comprise as many as 14 sections, must either be self-supporting once it is removed from the model, or have a support to keep the empty mold in position for pressing in the clay aggregate.

Where mold segments are not self-supporting, it is necessary to make a plaster jacket to hold the mold pieces in position while pressing in the clay. Self-supporting mold sections are held together with U-shaped metal clips called dogs while the clay is pressed in. The clay pieces are left to stiffen for about a week. This process is well described and illustrated in an article in *Ceramic Review* 165, 1997.

Aylieff uses Vingerling clays and various unrefined brick clays. The bright inclusions in the clay are made of fired, colored porcelains and two types of glass: borosilicate and ballontini. The firing of her large sculptures is extremely slow so as to drive out all moisture, and the final temperature reaches about 1868°F (1020°C). After firing, the surface of the sculpture is dull and rough, requiring finishing to bring up the colors. This is done by grinding and polishing using an electric grinder with diamond discs; it is water-fed to provide lubrication and cut out dust.

Aylieff does weathering trials on her work and some pieces are sealed with silicone sealant to waterproof them.

ALI JEFFERY (UK)

Where Aylieff is a potter who has become a sculptor, Ali Jeffery is a sculptor who uses fired clay as her medium. She has been involved with clay since she was a child making things out of the clay she collected from the river at the bottom of her garden. Her sculptures are inspired by her enjoyment of the countryside and the natural world. She makes sculptures which have organic shapes and allude to natural forms without being representational. It is important to her that her work is set in the open as she makes large pieces and aims to create a strong presence with them.

Ideas for her work emerge gradually through drawings she makes from her imagination. The objects she collects during walks on beaches or in the countryside provide visual references for her sculptures.

Jeffery likes both the tactile qualities of clay and the challenge of making large-scale pieces. She uses heavily grogged clays, such as Craft Crank or Raku body, and does not glaze her work. Instead, she creates a texture on the surface of her sculptures and occasionally applies body stains to create dry, earthy colors. The work is fired to 2192°F (1200°C). Jeffery uses firing as a means to make her work durable and permanent rather than for decorative purposes.

Techniques

Her vertical standing sculptures, which may be 117 in. (3 m) tall, are built from separate sections which she makes by coiling. The pieces are designed to fit snugly together and stack up on an internal metal support after firing. A disadvantage of this method is that the complete sculpture cannot be assembled until all the pieces have been fired and this means that any alterations are virtually impossible. While some adjustments to the fit of the sections can be made by trimming with an angle grinder, it is essential to make accurate models and allow enough time for a trial fitting of the sculpture before installing it in an exhibition.

Jeffery used to pay a welder to build the metal stands but now does the welding herself. The sculptures are resistant to weathering as long as water is unable to get into the structure. She fills any cracks with car body filler and seals the surface with masonry waterproofing liquid.

'Destination Tree' by Ali Jeffery, installed at the Harley Gallery.
Photo: Robin Parrish.

135

GORDON COOKE (UK)

Cooke's involvement with both ceramics and garden design has led him not only to make pots for plants but also to make sculptural forms for the garden. He has made some very tall forms for his own garden, and the obelisk illustrated here was built in stacking sections, each of which was fired individually before being assembled outside.

'Obelisk' by Gordon Cooke. Stoneware.

CONCLUSION

The modern garden has stimulated a great diversity of ideas for potters and artists in clay. It has brought ceramic sculpture into the open air and started a renaissance in thrown plant pots and vases. Much of the work is modern in style, yet it continues a long tradition of pottery and ornament in gardens. Technological developments, such as studio kilns capable of firing to stoneware temperatures, have enabled many makers to develop work which is durable enough to survive the rigors of open-air locations.

Some of the potters in this book seek to preserve old methods and traditions, notably those who make terracotta plant pots, and they have been very selective in adopting modern methods. They may use power wheels or computerized controllers on their kilns, but only as long as the technology does not compromise the character of the pots they make. While some of these makers work on their own, others, such as Jim Keeling at Whichford Pottery, have set up small factories. The pots produced at Whichford are handmade yet standardized, and the working methods are similar to those of small local potteries prior to the Industrial Revolution. The potters of the past would not have shied away from any new technology which would enable them to produce greater quantities of more uniform pots.

Trends in garden and landscape design have stimulated a demand for interesting garden ornamentation. Potters have responded by producing a great variety of individual and original work. Many of the potters in this book have adapted their working methods to cope with the technical demands of making large pieces, and they have devised many clever strategies for dealing with heavy weights and bulky forms.

Ceramics is increasingly being used to make sculpture for gardens, and while abstract sculpture is well represented in ceramics, there is also a movement towards figurative work – previously the domain of sculptors working in metal, stone or wood.

In this book I have illustrated some of the great variety of work being produced by contemporary artists and potters. I hope that by reading about some of their techniques, others will see that it is possible to make large pieces without the need to be heroically strong or to invest in a lot of expensive machinery. If my book manages to inspire more artists to make ceramics for the open air, or to alert gardeners and designers to the beautiful and exciting ceramics currently available, then it will have succeeded in its purpose.

PRACTICAL CONSIDERATIONS

A. FROST AND WEATHER RESISTANCE

Resistance to the effects of weather and frost has to be given serious consideration if work is to be kept permanently out in the open. If water penetrates or pools in a clay object and freezes, the pressure of the expanding ice causes the piece to crack. The entire pot or sculpture may crack, or parts of the surface chip away. With chipping, the piece gradually loses more and more of the surface with each successive frost and it will eventually disintegrate. Coarse, porous clays which allow water to soak into the fabric of the pot are more liable to chip, whereas smooth clays run a higher risk of cracking apart.

Potters and artists working with fired clay have two main strategies for avoiding frost damage. One is to fire the clay body to its vitrification point which closes the tiny pores in the clay and makes it impermeable to water. The second is to glaze the work, which helps to waterproof the clay by providing a glassy impermeable coat. However, where dry matt glazes are used on coarse, open-bodied clays, there may still be some residual porosity even after a stoneware firing.

Many artists use heavily grogged clays, as their robustness and strength make them suitable for building large pieces. These clays should be fired as high as possible if they are to be left

OPPOSITE: Group of terracotta flower pots in the Tradescant Garden, Lambeth, London.
Photo: Robin Parrish.

unglazed. Monica Young, who uses Craft Crank without glaze, recommends firing it to at least 2372°F (1300°C).

Such high firing temperatures may not be practical for all potters because of the different clay bodies they use, or the capabilities of their kilns. Designing shapes that drain easily prevents water from collecting where it could freeze. Planters that contain soil which could become waterlogged should be shaped so that the wet soil has room to expand if it freezes. This is why many plant pots are wider at the top than at the base. Jar shapes with shoulders and narrow openings are more at risk of frost damage than a conventional bucket shaped pot.

Some of the artists featured in this book leave their work unglazed for aesthetic reasons, and this means that it is not watertight. Some very open bodied clays with dry matt glazes may still remain porous even after firing to stoneware temperatures. If the clay cannot be fired to vitrification, potters can take advantage of modern water sealant fluids which are commonly used in the building trade. These sealants are based on silicone which is hydrophobic and repels water; hence their use in injecting bricks to make impermeable damp courses in buildings. One or more coats of the fluid can be painted on to a porous clay object, soaking in and sealing the pores. The clay is sealed when drops of water remain as round beads instead of spreading out and soaking into the surface.

Frost is the most obvious weather risk, but water collecting on the surface of a piece can cause growths of algae and moss which will eventually erode certain types of clay. Water migrating from the soil in a terracotta plant pot can cause salts to leach out and be deposited on the surface of the pot, which some people consider unsightly. For all these reasons, potters take a great deal of care in choosing suitable clays and working methods.

Wind is also a hazard for certain pieces and this is dealt with by suitable methods of installation. Techniques for securing work against buffeting winds are described in the section on installation.

B. DEALING WITH WEIGHT

Much ceramic work intended for the open air is large and heavy. Even modest-sized pieces such as window boxes or plant pots have to be robust enough to withstand the inevitable knocks that they will sustain when in use. While these may be heavy in proportion to their size, they are relatively easy to move and lift into kilns.

Large sculptural pieces are not only heavy but often bulky and complex in shape which makes them difficult to maneuver, and they may not easily fit into the kiln. Potters have developed various means of resolving these problems and often use a combination of methods. There are several main strategies for managing large and heavy work:

• Make the work from small, manageable modules which can be assembled after firing to build a single large form. This method has been adopted by many makers and is well illustrated by Holly Hanessian assembling a birdbath (see Chapter 5).

•Ensure that the work bench or base, any trolleys or carts, and the kiln shelf, are all at the same level, as it is easier to push heavy pieces around on boards than it is to lift them. Thomas Gale, Jennifer Jones, Jean Lowe and Jim Robison use variations of this method combined with the use of trolleys.

• Use wheels. Many of the makers in this book have trolleys for moving pieces around their workshops. Some, like Cameron Williams and Monica Young, have the use of heavier equipment such as forklifts and hoists, and move their very large works on batts or pallets.

• Employ assistants.

• Instead of trying to put very big works into a kiln, several potters construct their kilns over their pots. A good example of this approach is Christine-Ann Richards (Chapter 6) whose photographs show how she builds her big pots inside a top-hat kiln.

Below is a description of how five potters overcome potential problems with the weight of their work.

Jean Lowe starts her sculptures on her work bench, constructing them on octagonal pieces of blockboard or plywood 0.8 in. (2 cm) thick. When the work is about 24 in. (60 cm) high it is lifted on its board down to a low trolley where it is then completed to its full height. The trolley helps in moving the piece from work station to the kiln. Her sculpture is wheeled up to the kiln floor of the large trolley kiln and, on its board, it is carefully lifted on to the kiln shelf. This usually requires three or four people each taking a corner of the board. Once the sculpture is on the kiln trolley, two people quickly lift it while Lowe takes away the wooden board. The helpers gently lower the sculpture back on to the kiln floor. To reduce the risk of cracking around the base of the piece during firing, she spreads sand on the kiln floor.

Storage of the sculptures during the lengthy drying period can be a problem in a communal studio where space is shared, so a trolley is used to move the sculpture to an interim storage facility outside the studio. Once the piece has been glazed and fired it is moved out of the studio.

OPPOSITE: Group of 'Pebble' forms by Jean Lowe on the shore of the Medway estuary, Kent.

Step 1: The sculpture on its board is wheeled to the kiln on a low trolley. *All photos: Jola Spytkowska.*

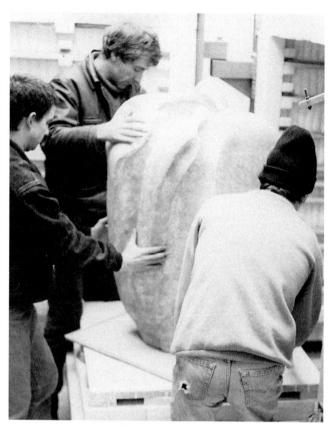

Step 2: Two people lift the sculpture while the third person removes the wooden board.

Step 3: Jean Lowe pushes the kiln trolley and sculpture into the kiln.

Step 4: The sculpture inside the kiln just before the kiln door is closed.

Jenifer Jones finds that moving her pots around the studio and getting them into the kiln can be a problem but, by keeping pots at a constant level when working, she is able to maneuver fairly large pieces without needing the strength to lift them. She makes each pot on a board on a wooden base which is at the same level as the kiln floor, and uses a trolley to move the pot to the kiln. When the pot is dry she pushes it on its board from the base to the trolley, wheels it across to the kiln and then pushes the pot on to the kiln shelf. She has several bases of the right height. The trolley is made from a wooden box with a set of wheels.

Jim Robison moves pieces of sculpture on boards and they are brought up to the level of the kiln shelf before loading. Sometimes the object is constructed on a piece of cardboard on a wooden board. Sand is applied to the kiln shelf so that the whole piece on its cardboard can be slid into position. The cardboard protects the base and edges of the work and is left to burn away in the firing. Sometimes he uses pieces of wooden dowel as rollers to move heavy pieces around the studio.

Felicity Aylieff and **Ian Gregory.** Aylieff sometimes uses an engine crane and forklift to extract the clay sculpture from the mold when the weight exceeds 220 lb. (100 kg). She has a large kiln and uses the forklift and crane for moving pieces around. Ian Gregory uses a forklift to move heavy work around, and he has a trolley kiln. He also constructs his ceramic fiber flat-pack kilns around the biggest sculptures.

Coiled urn with radial scoring by Jenifer Jones. D. 17.5 in. (45 cm).

C. INSTALLATION AND SAFETY NOTES

There are several factors which have to be taken into account when installing large pieces of ceramic sculpture. It is important that the work is securely fixed for the following reasons:

- The item has to be secure enough not to pose any risk of falling and injuring people
- The piece has to stand firmly, as fired clay crumbles easily and it could break if it toppled
- The work has to withstand buffeting by strong winds
- It has to be secured against the possibility of theft
- There is the risk of vandalism or knocks if installed in a public space

Moving the work to the site has to be planned. Installation of heavy pieces can be a problem, so Monica Young, for example, provides strong nets which act as slings, allowing pots to be carried over rough ground and hoisted into place. She makes a hole in the center of the base of a pot if it is to be fixed to the ground. Jean Lowe uses plenty of pieces of hardboard, foam sponges and old pillows to slide her sculptures into the back of an estate car.

The process of installation must also be thoroughly planned. Special equipment, such as a forklift or crane, may be required to put the work into position. If the piece is to be mounted on a wall, or is very tall, a scaffold tower may be necessary. Builders or welders may have to be employed to install the work. How this is organized has to be discussed and arranged in advance with the client.

It is important to find out whether there are factors which may cause unexpected problems with installation. The site must be checked carefully and arrangements made to deal with any problems. For example, the wall on which a mural is to be attached may need repair and special paving or a base may be required for a free-standing piece.

Many artists have devised techniques for securing their work against theft or damage. One method is a spike with a horizontal bar attached driven into the ground through an enlarged drain hole in a plant con-

tainer. Another is to fit metal collars to large pots so that they can be fixed to an adjacent wall. Many potters, such as John Cliff and Andrea Wulff, rely on the weight of the pots when filled with earth and plants. Large decorative empty jars may be filled with sand. Jonathan Garratt sometimes drills a pair of holes near the base of his pots through which he passes a strong wire. He uses an ordinary electric drill with a sharp masonry bit to make fixing holes in his pots. He uses the drill at standard speed only, because the hammer action could crack the pot. He can then padlock the pot to a stake in the ground.

Stage 1. Jim Robison's installation begins with excavation for a base slab. This has been maneuvered into position on a trolley. A threaded bar has been secured to the base through a hole drilled in the slab and fixed with retaining nuts and washers both above and below the slab.

Stage 2. The base slab is in position and leveled and the sculpture is lifted on to the threaded bar. Robison uses a tractor, trailer and foam padding for transporting the work to the site.

Jim Robison has had a lot of experience in making public sculptures and has had to take all of the above factors into account. His large sculptures are often made for public commissions won through competitions and they require secure mounting. Since strong winds can be more of a risk to a garden sculpture than vandalism, he uses concrete or stone flags as anchor points for the base and the work is bolted down. Tall pieces made from stacking modules are mounted on a threaded bar fixed into the base. Work for public parks is filled with concrete and wall panels or tiles are bedded in cement. He uses a scaffold and the aid of assistants when installing large sculptures made from several stacking pieces.

RIGHT: Stage 3. The top section of the sculpture 'Winter Figure' is in place, secured by a retaining nut and washer inside the work. This is reached through a removable lid or cap on top of the work which can be glued in place later. Sometimes a bead of silicone mastic is used between sections to give some cushion and room for movement. It is important not to overtighten the retaining rod as it will expand and contract at a faster rate than the ceramic sections of the sculpture.

Ali Jeffery working on 'Destination Tree' sculpture.

Central pole (1.65 in. diameter, 71 in. long) passing through segments and visible in places.

Metal base, about 16 ft. (5m) diameter and H-shaped to support the structure and allow it to be freestanding.

Method of attachment. A metal sleeve fits into the pole and it is fastened by a grub screw. The sleeve sits in a recess in the ceramic section so it is not visible.

Diagram of installation of 'Destination Tree' sculpture by Ali Jeffery.

Ali Jeffery's work is always very securely installed, not just to prevent theft or vandalism, but also for public safety. Her sculptures are usually mounted on metal posts on a base. If a sculpture is to be located outside, the metal base can be buried in the ground or bolted on to concrete. She makes allowances for this in the design of the stand.

Christine-Ann Richards uses bolts to fix large pots such as her 'Wave Form' to the ground or base. She uses 1–1.25 in. (2.5–3 cm) galvanized

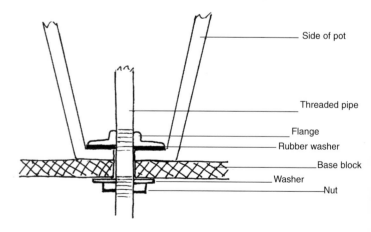

Side of pot

Threaded pipe

Flange
Rubber washer
Base block
Washer
Nut

Diagram showing Christine-Ann Richards' method of fixing tall pots to the ground.

part-threaded piping obtained from agricultural suppliers. The flanged nuts are tightened on the threaded pipe with a large spanner to secure the bottom of the pot to the base slab.

Jean Lowe's work is robust and will withstand small children climbing into the hollows without damage. For work in public places, she always recommends that the piece is plugged and bolted to a stone, brick or concrete slab to prevent theft. Her glazes are

'Wave: Earth 1' by Christine-Ann Richards. H. 45 in. (1.15 m). *Photo: Sally Pollitzer.*

unaffected by solvents or detergents used for removing spray paint, tar or similar substances, so the sculpture can be cleaned.

D. COMMISSIONS AND CONTRACTS

Many of the artists in this book work to commission because of the large scale of their work. Those who work on a smaller scale, or who produce large numbers of pots of the same shape, may find undertaking a commission fairly straightforward, as the client has usually seen something that the artist already makes and has ordered a similar piece. These artists rarely have to negotiate a special contract for a commission.

Birdbath by Gordon Broadhurst, stoneware clay with barium glazes and slips. H. 47 in. (1.2 m).

Often the client will decide where to place the piece in their garden, and no special fixings will be needed.

However, arrangements should be agreed with the client and put in writing. Details concerning payment, delivery dates and installation should be set out in a letter. Many commissions require specific work for a particular setting, whether in a private or public location and, in this case, many factors have to be taken into account. A site visit and preliminary notes, drawings and designs are essential. The cost of these should be added into the final price of the work.

The way in which Gordon Broadhurst approaches commissions covers some of the most important points. He points out that designing and making ceramic artifacts and structures for the garden or landscaped environment can be very challenging. It involves having to resolve a number of technical, physical and logistical problems.

The scale of the work to be made has to be considered. Scale is a factor which can easily be overlooked. Where a commission is for small scale or domestic ceramics, problems with scaling up a design rarely have to be taken into account. However, many designs do not automatically translate neatly into large pieces. Significant changes take place when enlarging from a scale model and this will affect the production time and cost of the materials.

An example would be in scaling up a cube with sides 39 in. (1 m) in length. This cube holds 35 cu. ft. (1 m³). Its surface area is 64 sq. ft. (6 m²) and the distance round is 156 in. (4 m). If the cube was doubled in size so that each side was 78 in. (2 m) long, it would have a volume of 282 cu. ft. (8 m³) (eight times greater). The surface area would be 258 sq. ft. (24 m²) (four times greater) and the distance around it would be 312 in. (8 m) (two times greater). If the thickness of the material was also doubled to support the extra size, then the second cube would be eight times heavier than the first one. In other words, doubling the height of a piece will more than double the work and costs involved in making it. Certain factors, therefore, need to be considered:

• Will it be a one-off piece or multiples?

• What are the most appropriate production methods? Can existing skills be adapted or do new techniques have to be learned?

• Will there be access to appropriate equipment such as extra large kilns or lifting equipment?

Occasionally a commission may be too large for the artist to construct in their own studio or kiln. Both Jenifer Jones and Gwen Heeney have made arrangements to work in factories to produce large commissions, while John Cliff rented an extra large studio for an architectural commission. He also worked in Cameron Williams' studio when they collaborated on a commission for very large pots.

Communicating with the client is important. Presenting the client with a range of drawings and models of proposed ideas helps to establish what is required and avoids any ambiguities and future difficulties. It also enables artists to organize their thoughts, anticipate any problems, and consider appropriate solutions before communicating these to the client.

Large-scale commissions may require advance payments to cover the costs of preliminary designs, models and purchase of materials. There may be other costs, such as paying for assistants or hiring space in larger studios and kilns. For such commissions a proper written contract between the maker and the client is essential.

Contracts

Depending on the nature of the commission, a contract may be a simple letter or a detailed document. However, it should cover both parties and all the following points:
1. Description of the work to be made.
2. The price and arrangements for payment of a deposit (typically between 10% and 50% of the total), interim payments and the final payment.
3. Delivery arrangements and completion times.
4. Responsibility for the costs of preliminary designs or other costs such as photography of the finished work.
5. Installation details.
6. Copyright.
7. Responsibility for work not carried out by the artist. This may be arranging for a builder to prepare the site, or install the work, or where any other person such as a metalworker or garden designer is involved. The organization and allocation of these responsibilities should be thoroughly discussed in advance and approved by both the client and the artist.
8. Responsibility for safety aspects if the work is in a public place.
9. Insurance. If the work is for a temporary exhibition in a gallery it is important to establish whether the gallery is insured. If it is not insured, prior agreement must be made about compensation for any loss or damage during the exhibition.
10. Information for the client about care and maintenance of the work, fragility, method of cleaning and how to package it properly if necessary.
11. Disputes and their resolution.

Late payment is a problem that should be considered, and it is advisable to include a reminder that the work remains the property of the artist until the final payment has been made.

Some public commissions are obtained through competitions, where the artist has to submit a proposal. The cost of preparing the designs and models should be built in to the price of the commissioned work, but there is usually no provision for the design costs of those who are unsuccessful.

The artists below provide examples of what may be involved in working on commission:

Patricia Volk usually works with a specific exhibition or gallery in mind. All payment is then handled by the gallery concerned, usually with 50% in advance, and the remainder on delivery.

Security against theft or damage is the responsibility of the buyer or gallery, and Volk advises all artists and craftspeople to deal only with galleries which are properly insured.

Her most recent commission for a site-specific installation came about through an arts consultant. The commission was confirmed with a contract, there was a 50% advance payment, and the remainder was paid on completion. Even so, she

Detail of 'Deity' by Patricia Volk. 19.5 in. (50 cm).

found that she had done a substantial amount of work before receiving the first check. Her contract was a variation on the standard Arts Council contract which covers most of the points listed above.

Kate Malone A client may have a pond or patio that they ask her to look at. She then develops specific ideas which may be suggested by the history of the site, or by certain flowers or shrubs nearby. Malone takes great care over the siting of the work. If the work is not well sited and level it will not look its best, regardless of its visual qualities. She reminds others not to overlook practicalities, such as whether the ground will withstand the weight of a large work.

John Cliff finds that working on a commission basis is very different from working as a production and exhibiting potter. In most cases, the design is decided in consultation with the client: this may be a single individual or members of a committee. This consultation takes the form of meetings about the site, the aesthetics, function and cultural or social requirements of the commission. The design may also be affected by building codes, fire regulations, cleaning requirements or portability. All this might seem to compromise the overall aesthetics, but can also act as a challenge and catalyst for new ways of working.

Sarah Walton has a different approach. She prefers to give clients a choice of different pieces from existing designs.

BIBLIOGRAPHY

Adams, William Howard   *Nature Perfected: Gardens Through History* (Abbeville Press, 1991)
'Andrea Wulff' (*Neue Keramik* No 5, Sept/Oct 1996)
Ariail, Kate 'Holly Hanessian' (*Ceramics Monthly*, March 1996)
Aylieff, Felicity 'Larger than Life' (*Ceramic Review* No 165, 1997)

Balston, Michael   *The Well Furnished Garden* (Mitchell Beazley)
Beckett; Carr; and **Stevens** *The Contained Garden* (Windward)
Bennett, Astrid Hilder 'David Dahlquist and Public Art' (*Ceramics Monthly*, October 1993)
Boursnell, Clive; **Cooper,** Guy; and **Taylor,** Gordon *English Water Gardens* (Weidenfeld & Nicholson, 1987)

'Cameron Williams' (*Pottery in Australia* No 31.3)
Caselles, Daniel and **Weissbuch,** Ellen 'Thrown Planters' (*Butlletí Informatiu de Ceràmica* No 54, 1994)
Cooke, Gordon 'Landscape, Colour and Clay' (*Ceramic Review* 135, 1992)

Daniel, Christopher St J. H. *Sundials* (Shire Publications,1997)
Demolliens, Jean-Luc and Emmanuelle 'Large Thrown Pots' (*Revue Céramique & Verre* No 85, 1995)

de Waal, Edmund 'Scorched Earth' (*Ceramic Review* 172, 1998)
Dolz, Dora 'Fountains and large scale sculptural work' (*Neue Keramik* 2/94)

France, Christine *Marea Gazzard +Form and Clay* (Art & Australian Books, 1994)

Gabsi, Margo 'Fountains and Architectural Ceramics' (*Pottery in Australia* No 32.2, 1993)
Gregory, Ian 'Flatpack Kilns' (*Ceramic Review* 172, 1998)
Gregory, Ian *Sculptural Ceramics* (A & C Black; Craftsman House; Overlook Press, 1997)

Heath, Jane; **Houston,** John; **Nuttgens,** Patrick; and **van den Broecke,** Floris *The Furnished Landscape: Applied Art in Public Places* (Bellew Publishing, 1992)
Heeney, Gwen 'Bench Mark' (*Ceramic Review* 173, 1998)
Hernandez, Celestino 'Eduardo Andaluz' (*Ceramics Monthly,* May 1995)
Hessenberg, Karin 'Five Women in the Garden' (*Ceramic Review* 137, 1992)
Hickey, Gloria 'Sadashi Inuzuka' (*Ceramics Monthly,* March 1994)
Hillier, Malcolm *Container Gardening* (Dorling Kindersley, 1991)
Huggins, John *Pots for Plants and Gardens* (Batsford, 1991)

'International Ceramics Symposium, Tashkent' (*Ceramics: Art & Perception* No 5, 1991)
'JoanCampbell' (*Pottery in Australia* No 31.4, 1992)
'John Cliff and Cameron Williams' (*Pottery in Australia* Vol 34.1, 1995)

Keeling, Jim *The Terracotta Gardener* (Headline, 1990)

Landsberg, Sylvia *The Medieval Garden* (British Museum Press, 1996)
Levi Marshall, Will 'In the Realm of the Senses' (*Ceramic Review* 162, 1996)
Lewis, Chris 'A Passion for Pots' (*Ceramic Review* 162, 1996)
Lucchesi, Bruno *Modelling the Head in Clay* (Pitman,1979)
L'Europe des Ceramistes, No 38 Mai 1989 (Centre Culturel de l'Yonne)

Madola Barcelona's 'Castilla Fountain' (*Ceramics Monthly*, March 1995)
Malone, Kate 'Crystalline Alchemy' (*Ceramic Review* 164,1997)
Mansfield, Janet *A Collector's Guide to Modern Australian Ceramics* (Craftsman House, 1988)
McHoy, Peter *Garden Ornaments and Statuary* (Ward Lock, 1987)

McKeown, Julie *Royal Doulton* (Shire Publications, 1997)

Neely, John 'The Wood Firer' (*Ceramics: Art & Perception* No 10, 1992)

Robison, Jim *Large Scale Ceramics* (A & C Black; Craftsman House, 1997)

Scharfe, Antje (*Neue Keramik* No 4 Summer,1996)
Schultz, Warren *City Gardens* (Merehurst Ltd)
Seisbøll, Lise 'Tommerupp – A Chapter in the History of Ceramic Art' (*Ceramics: Art & Perception* 34, 1998)
'Steffanie Samuels' (*Ceramics Monthly*, Summer 1993)
Strong, Roy *Small Period Gardens* (Conran Octopus, 1992)
Symes, Michael *Garden Sculpture* (Shire Publications, 1996)

'The Pottery at Relbia' (*Pottery in Australia* No 26.3, 1987)
Tolstrup, Lisbeth 'Dialectic Dialogue: Hans and Birgitte Börjeson' (*Ceramics: Art & Perception* No 10)

Valencia, Joe 'Maria Alquilar – A Perspective on Public Art' (*Ceramics Monthly*, May 1996)

GLOSSARY

Batt
1. Round wooden board which can be attached to a potter's wheel for making large pots which can then be lifted off using the board.
2. Alternative name for a kiln shelf.

Bisque
Preliminary firing before a glaze firing, usually carried out between 1832–2012°F (1000°–1100°C).

Blunger
Machine for stirring and mixing up slip.

Boss
Round decorative feature or knob added to a pot. See also *Sprig*.

Engobe
Another word for slip, or a slip-glaze.

Lute
A method in which clay slabs are joined by cross hatching the edges and using slip to stick them together.

Molochite
Calcined china clay which is used as an additive to clay bodies instead of ordinary china clay to minimize contraction during firing.

Natch
Small knob and socket made in adjacent edges of plaster mold sections to prevent them from slipping out of position.

Rococo
Type of elegant but light-hearted decoration fashionable in the 18th century, characterized by cherubs, flowers, butterflies and birds.

Roulette
An engraved wheel or cylinder which produces a repeat pattern when rolled over the clay.

Slump
The sag which occurs when a pot is over-fired.

Sprig
A small decorative feature made in a mold. It is then applied to the surface of a pot. See also *Boss*.

Swag
Type of decorative feature, usually a loop of drapery or foliage applied round the belly of an ornamental pot.

Temper
Material such as sand added to a clay body to open it and give it strength.

Terra sigillata
Very fine slip which produces an almost impermeable shiny surface on a pot.

Terracotta
Earthenware clay, usually red or buff.

Terrazzo
Clay with inclusions of glass or other types of previously fired, colored clay.

EXHIBITION VENUES

HERE IS A SELECTION OF GALLERIES WHICH SHOW THE WORK OF SOME OF THE ARTISTS IN THIS BOOK.

UNITED KINGDOM

The Garden Gallery
Rookery Lane
Broughton
STOCKBRIDGE
Hants SO20 8AZ

'Déjeuner sur l'Herbe' by Althea Wynne at The Garden Gallery.
Photo: Rachel Bebb.

The Harley Gallery
Welbeck
WORKSOP,
Notts S80 3LW

View of the courtyard exhibition area at the Harley Gallery

The New Arts Centre
Sculpture Park and Gallery
Roche Court
East Winterslow
SALISBURY
Wilts SP5 1BG

The Hannah Peschar Sculpture Garden
Black and White Cottage
Standon Lane
OCKLEY
Surrey RH5 5QR

OPPOSITE: Spiral form by Felicity Aylieff in the Hannah Peschar Sculpture Garden.
Photo: Hannah Peschar.

'Blue Event' by Derek Morris at the New Art Centre, Roche Court. Stoneware. H. 1.64 m (64 in).

The Scottish Gallery
16 Dundas Street
EDINBURGH EH3 6HZ

AUSTRALIA

Mura Clay Gallery
King Street
NEWTOWN 2042
NSW

DENMARK

Ceramic Museum of Grimmerhus
MIDDELFART
Funen

GERMANY
Galerie Latterman
DARMSTADT

HOLLAND
The Garden of Delight
Zuidbuurt 30
VLAARDINGEN
email: wdelight@xs4all.nl

USA
Old Town Gallery
P.O. Box 2521
PARK CITY
Utah 84060

Peter's Barn
Beck House
South Ambersham
MIDHURST
West Sussex GU29 0BX

View of the gardens at Peter's Barn Gallery with a group of 'Female Icons' by Mo Jupp.

USEFUL ADDRESSES

ARTISTS MENTIONED IN THIS BOOK CAN BE CONTACTED THROUGH THE FOLLOWING ORGANIZATIONS:

AUSTRALIA

Ceramics: Art and Perception
35 William Street
Paddington
NSW 2021
Tel. +612 9361 5286

The Potters' Society of Australia
PO Box 937
Crows Nest
NSW 2065

DENMARK

National Committee Denmark
c/o Dalhoff Larsens Fond
GI, Kongevej 124, IV
DK - 1850 Frederiksberg C
Tel. +45 31 31 61 26

FRANCE

Association Internationale du Nouvel
Objet Visuel
Catherine Brelet
27 Rue de l'Université
75005 Paris

Féderation Nationale des Ateliers
d'Art
Poulcot
56520 Guidel
Tel. +33 97 65 31 87

Guide des Céramistes
Editions de la Revue de la Céramique
et du Verre
61 Rue Marconi, BP 3
62880 Vendin le Vieil

GERMANY

Bundesverband Kunsthandwerk
Berufsverband handwerk Kunst
Design
eV
Rheinstrasse 23
D-60325 Frankfurt/ Main
Tel. +49 697 402 31

Verlag Neue Keramik Gmbh
Unter den Eichen 90
D-12205 Berlin

UNITED KINGDOM

The Arts Council of England
14 Great Peter Street
London SW1P 3NQ
Tel. 0171 333 0100

The Crafts Council
44A Pentonville Road
London N1 9BY
Tel. 0171 278 7700

The Craft Potters Association
William Blake House
7 Marshall Street
London W1V 1FD
Tel. 0171 437 7605

UNITED STATES OF AMERICA

The American Ceramic Society
PO Box 6136
Westerville
Ohio 43086-613

The American Crafts Council
72 Spring Street
New York
NY 10012
Tel. +1 212 274 0630

WEBSITES OF INTEREST

www.ceramicmill.com
www.ruffordceramiccentre.org.uk
www.vromansgallery.com

Many new websites come out each month, so it is worth a regular search under ceramics, clay, pottery, galleries, etc.

LIST OF SUPPLIERS

CERAMIC MATERIALS

UNITED KINGDOM

Bath Potters' Supplies
2 Dorset Close
Twerton
Bath BA2 3RF
Tel. 01225 337 046

Clayman
Morells Barn
Park Lane
Chichester
W. Sussex PO20 6LR
Tel. 01243 265 845

Potclays Ltd
Brickkiln Lane
Etruria
Stoke on Trent ST4 7BP
Tel. 01782 219 816

Potterycrafts Ltd
Campbell Road
Stoke on Trent ST4 4ET
Tel. 01782 645 000

NORTH AMERICA

Axner Pottery Supply
PO Box 621484
Oviedo
Florida 32765
USA
Tel. 800 843 7057

Mile Hi Ceramics Inc
77 Lipan Street
Denver
CO 80223
USA
Tel. 800 456 0163

Standard Ceramic Supply
P.O. Box 4435
Pittsburgh
PA 15205-0435
USA
Tel. 412 276 6333

Tucker's Pottery Supplies Inc.
15 West Pearce Street, Unit 7
Richmond Hill
Ontario L4B 1H6
Canada
Tel. 800 304 6185

AUSTRALIA

Pottery Supplies
262 Given Tee
Paddington
Brisbane, QD 4064
Tel. 07 36 3633

Venco Products
29 Owen Road
Kelmscott
Washington, WA 6111
Tel. 09 399 5265

Walker Ceramics
Boronia Road
Wantirna
Victoria 3125
Tel. 729 4755

PUMPS

Pumps can be obtained from all garden centers which deal with ponds and aquatics.

LETTERING

Hot metal type in any size or font at reasonable prices is obtainable from most foundries. A good supplier in the United Kingdom is:

Mouldtype Foundry
Dunkirk Lane
Leyland
Preston
Lancs. PR5 3BY
Tel. 01772 456 093

ACRYLICS AND VARNISHES

Acrylics and varnishes are obtainable from most art materials suppliers.

Patricia Volk uses 'Golden Varnishes', golden acrylics and mediums for painting which are obtainable from:

Atlantis Art Materials Limited
146 Brick Lane
London E1
Tel. 0171 377 8855

ADHESIVES AND SEALANTS

Liquid silicone sealant, sealant gel or paste, fillers and many adhesives such as Araldite, are obtainable from builders' merchants and hardware stores. 3M polystyrene adhesive is obtainable from:

3M at 3M House
Bracknell
Berks. RG12 1JU
Tel. 01344 858 000

Holly Hanessian uses PC-7 which is available in both black and white from hardware stores in the USA.

METAL RODS, NUTS AND BOLTS

Metal rods, nuts and bolts are available from most agricultural suppliers, industrial fixings suppliers, welders and blacksmiths.

INDEX